Sydney Harbour

The 'Europa' on Sydney Harbour.

For Oliver
and
Juliette

Published by
DAVID MESSENT PHOTOGRAPHY
Telephone Sydney 971 5970
First Edition Published 1994

Copyright
National Library of Australia
ISBN Number 0 646 17888 1

Text: David Messent
                        and David McGonigal
Editorial assistant: Denise Llewellyn
Production executive: Francoise Messent
Design consultant: Juliette Messent
Walks coordinator: Oliver Messent
Photography: David Messent
Helicopter flights: Sydney Helicopter Service
                        and Helicopter Charter
Maps: Universal Press Pty Ltd
Typesetting: Max Peatman
Assembly: Max Peatman

Separations by Sinnott Bros., Sydney
Printed in Singapore by Kyodo

Contents

Introduction

In the short space of two hundred years Sydney Harbour has been transformed from a dumping ground for convicts to which free settlers could only be enticed by a generous offer of free land grants to a sought after holiday and residential destination surrounded by the homes of over four million people.

By a stroke of good fortune much of the 160 kilometre shoreline of the Harbour hasn't been engulfed by residential and industrial development, but remains in its natural state for everyone to see and enjoy.

There are the towering breezy cliffs of North Head, which vie for space with the sultry tidal mangroves of Bantry Bay and the Lane Cove River. Quiet Harbour beaches like Cobblers and Collins, unchanged in appearance since the arrival of the First Fleet when Aborigines roamed the shore to prise oysters from the rocks and accessible only by bush track or boat, contrast with the busy seaside atmosphere of other Harbour beaches like Manly Cove and Balmoral where an ice cream or a meal of fish and chips is only a walk across the street away.

Gentle walks on well-graded sealed paths past orderly stands of tall Norfolk Island Pines and eucalypts on North Harbour and around the shore of Cremorne Point compare with rugged bush tracks following trails hemmed in by the impenetrable bush of Upper Middle Harbour and the Lane Cove River.

Guarding the approaches to the Harbour are Victorian forts hewn from solid sandstone with their cannons still resting gently on wooden carriages at Bradleys Head and Fort Denison. Within cannon-shot are the Harbour mansions of Vaucluse House and Elizabeth Bay House, and the man-made wonders of Sydney Opera House and Harbour Bridge. Further up the Harbour are the recreation facilities and museums of Darling Harbour, the workers terraces and cottages of Balmain, the industrial ghostlands of Cockatoo Island and Mortlake, the sports stadium and pool for the Sydney 2000 Olympics and Elizabeth Farm, the oldest house in Australia.

Harbourside parks with their own beaches like Clontarf and Nielsen Park have picnic tables and barbecues where you can watch the sailing boats drift by as the steak sizzles, or on more secluded reaches of the upper harbour, lush green lawns spill down to the water's edge at Tambourine Bay Reserve Riverview and Elkington Park Balmain. None of these though compare with the oldest and most beautiful of the Harbourside parks, that supreme example of the horticulturalist's art, the Sydney Royal Botanic Gardens.

For something quite different you can return to nature at the nudist beach of Lady Bay, or become a caste-away for the day at the parks on Clarke, Shark or Rodd Island, where on a week-day you'll probably find you have the whole island to yourself.

Whatever your creed or calling I trust this book will inspire visitors and locals to see and explore the Wonder of the World that is Sydney Harbour.

David Messent

Previous pages: The 'Crystal Harmony' off South Head on its way into Sydney Harbour.

Sydney Opera House and Harbour Bridge at dusk (left).

Harbour lookouts and quiet beaches

Spectacular views from North Head and a fascinating tour of the old buildings
of Manly Quarantine Station. Secluded Collins and Store Beaches on Spring Cove.
Sydney's most famous harbourside walk from Manly to The Spit Bridge, passing a
variety of scenery on the way including parks, beaches, coastal heathland, a pocket of
ancient forest and high sandstone ridges with panoramic harbour views.

North Head

There couldn't be a more logical place to start a tour of Sydney Harbour than with the sheer sandstone cliffs of North Head, standing like an impenetrable citadel guarding the north entrance of the harbour.

From Manly town centre, the long straight hill of Darley Road leads through Manly's suburban houses, past Manly Hospital, to North Head Scenic Drive, which continues for two kilometres through bushland to a car park on the headland. From here a circular walking track about a kilometre long winds through the heathland on the Head, past one or two concrete lookouts constructed during the Second World War to keep a watch for enemy shipping, to a series of lookouts on the south side of the head, with views across the entrance of the harbour to South Head and straight down the harbour to the city. North Head is the highest and most spectacular lookout of all the reserves on the harbour fore-shores, and provides a good vantage point for viewing the entry to Sydney of the world's great ocean liners, and naval ships.

The walk was created by John Fairfax and Sons owners of the Sydney Morning Herald in 1981 to mark the 150th anniversary of first publication of the Sydney Herald on April 18 1831.

Manly Quarantine Station

Returning to Manly, as North Head Scenic Drive makes a sharp turn to the right, on the left is the entrance to Manly Quarantine Station. Daytime tours of the station or a nightime 'ghost tour' can be arranged on most days through the New South Wales National Parks and Wildlife Service. There are no parking facilities at the station entrance, so tours start by bus at the terminal at Manly Wharf.

About 60 buildings remain at the Quarantine Station out of the 90 or so that used to occupy the 27 hectare site, most of them dating from the period when the station saw it's heaviest use from the 1870's to the 1920's.

The Station was first set aside as a quarantine area in 1828, when the convict transport *Bussorah Merchant* arrived in Sydney carrying smallpox. The convicts and their guards were unloaded at Store Beach with some tents and provisions where they were left to fend for themselves for a few weeks, while the crew and some free settlers were confined on board while the ship was moored in Neutral Bay.

The journey by sea to Sydney was longer than the incubation period of all known infectious diseases, including typhus, scarlet fever, smallpox and influenza. If a ship was a carrier of disease it would break out on board ship, so by careful quarantine

procedures authorities hoped to prevent the devastating effects of the various epidemics that frequently swept the European and Asian mainland. Initially facilities at the station were rough and ready and inmates were left to fend for themselves from stores that were dumped with them on the beach. They prepared their own food, pitched their own tents and were expected to clear the bush and work on the construction of permanent buildings. Conditions gradually improved while provision for accommodation kept pace with the passenger carrying capacity of ocean liners, so that by 1915 the Quarantine Station could comfortably accommodate over 1,500 souls.

On arrival at the station jetty, passengers showered in a dilute phenol solution, then dressed in clothes they had previously selected for treatment that had been sterilised in the station's steam rooms or 'autoclaves'. Some passengers who may have been in contact with disease carriers went through a horrifying (and as it was later discovered completely useless) procedure where they were shut in a room for ten minutes to inhale zinc sulphate gas in an attempt to kill evil 'miasmas' that may linger in their lungs. Shipping companies bringing a ship to Sydney carrying disease were deemed responsible for any quarantine costs incurred on arrival in port, and not only paid the expenses of the station, but housed

passengers in a similar style to that they'd enjoyed on board ship, waited on by the ship's crew who also cooked their meals. Areas of the station were separated into First, Second, Third and 'Asiatic' class accommodation, each with their own restaurants, lounges and sleeping quarters. Passengers fortunate enough not to be carrying disease themselves made the most of their enforced detention, playing cricket or tennis, swimming on Store Beach, wandering the bushland of North Head or walking to the lookout of 'Old Man's Hat' on the south side of the Head. Others set to work carving momentoes of their stay on the numerous sandstone rocks above the beaches or in the surrounding bush. There are hundreds of these carvings, over a thousand have been documented and many hundreds more lie uncatalogued on rocks now overgrown by bushland. Some are little more than scratchings on the rock, others look very professional and were executed by stonemasons who

travelled out as immigrants. They are the most poignant reminder of life on the station and range from sad epitaphs written by relatives for loved ones lost on the voyage out, to jolly tales of living conditions at the station. There's a memorial to the *William Rodger*, which arrived in 1838, losing 16 to disease on the voyage out and a further 29 at the station. William Usherwood inscribed his thoughts on stone in 1853, lamenting 'Oh misery of miseries, surely Job can never have been in quarantine.' A message on a rock next to the 'Asiatic' quarters has been translated from Chinese, and runs in part, '...I can only weep sadly to the moon, separated from my parents by vast oceans, whose love I have not reciprocated until this day', while a sailor inscribed in 1935, 'Oh to be in quarantine, now that summer's here, phoning up your friends at work, sending out for beer. Bathe by day and bridge by night, life of endless play. Oh to be in quarantine, banking up your pay.'

North Head (previous pages on right of picture) dominates the entrance to Sydney Harbour. Captain Collins of the Marines who travelled out with the First Fleet wrote of it as 'this noble and capacious harbour, equal if not superior to any yet known in the world.'

Fighter planes crowd the deck of the American aircraft carrier U.S.S. Independence (above) as she enters the harbour on a courtesy visit in 1992. The photograph was taken from the lookout at North Head.

Quarantine procedures were in general successful in keeping infectious diseases out of Sydney, however sometimes it was necessary to confine Sydney residents at the station, as happened during an outbreak of smallpox in 1881 and an outbreak of Bubonic plague in 1900. The smallpox outbreak of 1881 was caused by

the release of a man from quarantine, who was wrongly diagnosed with chicken pox when he in fact had a case of mild smallpox, while the plague was carried by the fleas on rats escaping ashore from ships docked in Sydney. Facilities at the station were stretched to the limit during the horrifying influenza epidemic of 1918-19. Stringent efforts had been made to prevent the disease getting ashore in Sydney; the Quarantine Station was filled to capacity and troop ships returning from the First World War stayed lying at anchor in the harbour with the soldiers confined on board. However the flu broke out in Melbourne and though ships arriving from Melbourne were quarantined in Sydney and police closed the New South Wales border with Victoria, a carrier somehow slipped through and Sydney suffered with the rest of the world with a virus that killed tens of millions around the globe.

The Station was only in occasional use after the 1930's. During the Second World War British evacuee children were temporarily housed there on arrival and the Station was used as a billet for soldiers. After the war one of the buildings was converted to a Commonwealth Detention Centre for illegal immigrants. The

Virgin bush (left) coats the rugged sandstone landscape of the south side of North Head. The area in the foreground was once part of Manly Quarantine Station, and a section of the old sandstone wall that enclosed the station can be seen as a white line in the bush in the middle distance on the left.

Station's final call to fame was in 1974, when 750 residents from Darwin were temporarily housed there after cyclone Tracy devastated the town on Christmas Day. Ten years later in 1984 the Station was closed for quarantine purposes completely, and assumed its present status as a historic sight, run by the National Parks and Wildlife Service.

A tour of the Station today around the deserted buildings with their wide shady verandahs, evokes a strange feeling of another time and place. The old sleeping quarters, dining rooms and lounges dating to the turn of the century are furnished in the style of the early 1950's from the time the Commonwealth Government last refurbished the station. Hospital beds from the same era stand neatly against the walls in the Quarantine Station Hospital as if the patients have just left them, and in the morgue medical glass jars and test-tubes line the shelves as if in wait for the ministrations of the pathologists.

Collins Beach

Continue on North Head Scenic Drive after the Quarantine Station, passing on the right North Head Army Barracks and School of Artillery, (which has an artillery museum in the grounds). After a few hundred metres turn right into Collins Beach Road, which winds down through a dense pocket of bushland to the Australian Police College. From a parking place on the right just before the college, a path leads through the bush to Collins Beach. (The Beach is also accessible by a path leading from Stuart Street on the other side). Collins Beach, named after Captain David Collins, Judge Advocate with the First Fleet, is a lovely quiet beach surrounded by natural bushland, the peaceful atmosphere enhanced by the sound of a small waterfall cascading over rocks at the southern end. The scene is no doubt little different today to the appearance of the Beach on 7

September 1790 when Phillip met the Aborigine Bennelong here after receiving from him a gift of meat from a dead whale. Bennelong was an Aborigine who Phillip had captured earlier at Manly, and brought back to Sydney to live with him, who'd recently escaped and made his way back to Manly. As Phillip was talking with Bennelong, another aborigine approached. When Phillip moved towards him, he threw his spear, which pierced Phillip through the shoulder. Lieutenant Henry Waterhouse, midshipman from the *Sirius*, broke the spear off at the shaft, and Phillip was rowed back to Sydney with his shoulder bleeding heavily from the wound. Fortunately the wound wasn't as serious as it first appeared, Phillip was operated on to remove the barb and he was up and about again ten days later. It's a mark of his character that he insisted no retaliation should be taken against the offending aborigine.

Store Beach

From the south end of Collins Beach it's a 10 minute clamber over the rocks at low tide to Store Beach. The beach was named for the stores that were left there for the early inmates of the Quarantine Station. In the later days of the Station in the early twentieth century, the beach was a popular 'resort' for First and Second Class passengers under temporary confinement at the Station. Just to remind them that it wasn't all for fun was a prominent notice on the beach, 'trespassers will be prosecuted, Penalty £25'. A path now completely overgrown by bush, used to lead from the Station to the beach. On the rocks above the beach are some carvings made by the Station inmates, while at the east end of the beach is the remains of the jetty used for dropping off the 'stores'.

Little Manly Cove

Little Manly Point west of Spring Cove was the site of a gasworks which was demolished in 1971. Manly

Council did sterling work to convert the former industrial wasteland into a park. The nearby sandy beach of Little Manly Cove, which has its own netted off swimming area and a kiosk open at weekends and on holidays, was named to differentiate it from the much larger Manly Cove around the corner, (called Big Manly Cove on early maps.).

Manly

Manly itself was named by Phillip before it's much better known cousin Sydney further up the harbour. After entering Sydney Harbour on January 21 1788 and spending the night at Camp Cove, Phillip's longboats started exploring the harbour shoreline the following morning. According to Phillip's dispatches to England, on January 22 1788:

'The boats in passing near a point of land in the harbour were seen by a number of men and 20 of them waded into the water unarmed, received what was offered to them and examined the boats with a curiosity that gave me a much higher opinion of them... and their confidence and manly bearing made me give the name of Manly Cove to this place.'

Phillip's narrative continued, 'the same people afterwards joined us when we dined' and because of 'their lively curiosity' Phillip drew a circle in the sand and instructed them to stay outside it.

The following day Phillip went on to discover and name Sydney Cove.

The first land grants in Manly were in 1810, but the area remained little more than a fishing village surrounded by bushland until the 1850's when Henry Gilbert Smith, a merchant and banker, inspired by Brighton from his native Sussex in England, developed 120 acres of land he owned in Manly. Smith erected a ferry wharf at Manly Cove, built a hotel nearby and cleared the bush from the wharf through to the ocean beach 500 metres away, to form a road he called 'The Corso' after a street in Rome. Advertising his creation with the slogan 'There is nothing like it in the wide wide world' and with tents where refreshments were served, a public bathhouse, maze, gardens, swings, walks and a ferry service to bring day-trippers from Sydney, Smith had turned Manly into a resort 60 years before Bondi became popular.

The walk to The Spit

Manly Wharf is the starting point for one of the best harbourside walks in Sydney, following the shoreline for nine kilometres to The Spit Bridge, three and a half hours and ten kilometres away. It is one of the most varied walks on Sydney Harbour, passing quiet beaches surrounded by bushland, modern harbourside suburbs, aboriginal sites, and untouched bush environments of coastal heathland, eucalypt forest and pockets of sub-tropical rain-forest. All along the way there are sweeping views of Sydney Harbour, particularly magnificent from the top of Dobroyd Head where a lookout gives a panoramic view of the majestic entrance to Sydney Harbour.

From the west side of Manly Wharf, follow the promenade along Manly Cove Beach past the netted off swimming pool, Manly Art Gallery and Museum and Oceanworld Aquarium to Manly Pier Seafood Restaurant. The restaurant, once owned by the Port Jackson and Manly Steamship Company that operated the Manly Ferries, was linked to Manly Wharf by a wooden promenade across the water of Manly Cove that fenced in a large shark proof swimming area. During a storm of almost hurricane force in 1974 the walkway was smashed to matchwood by the high seas.

Fairlight Beach

The path continues on a well-maintained walkway as it winds and undulates through the pine trees past Delwood and Fairlight Beach.

Fairlight Beach and the neighbouring suburb were named after Fairlight House, built on Eastern Hill Manly by Henry Gilbert Smith in 1854. The house itself was demolished to make way for a block of flats in 1939 and all that remains are remnants of the garden, a stone wall, and three Norfolk Island Pines. A stone kangaroo Smith had carved on a rock by the sculptor Percy Pickering still exists today near Ivanoe Park.

As the track approaches North Harbour Reserve, a small plaque erected by Manly Historical Society marks the spot where it is thought Phillip set out on April 15th 1788 to carry out his first exploration north of the Harbour. During an expedition that lasted three days, Phillip headed north, then west, pushing a way through the bush to Middle Harbour, (see also chapter 2).

North Harbour Reserve, with its picnic area and playing ground stands on five acres that were reclaimed from the mudflats at the head of North Harbour in 1938. From North Harbour Street above the reserve a wooden footbridge built by the Balgowlah Progress Association in 1918 crosses over a shady gully to a pocket of thickly forested bushland at Wellings Reserve. In the 1880's two Aboriginal skeletons were discovered in the woods in stone lined graves. The reserve is named after Leslie Wellings, a noted local historian and former Town Clerk of Manly.

Forty Baskets Beach

The track runs close to the shoreline, at first along a road, then on a path for a few hundred metres to Forty Baskets Beach, named for a catch of forty baskets of fish caught off the Beach sent to a contingent of New South Wales Troops from the Sudan detained at the Quarantine Station in 1885. After the wreck of the *Dunbar* on South Head in 1857, (see chapter 7) a Bible from the ship washed up on the Beach.

Reef Beach

A spur off the main track leads to Reef Beach. Unofficially a nudist beach until 1975, officially a nudist beach 1976-1993 and now unofficially a nudist beach again following pressure from residents living nearby, one of whom apparently once applied for a gun licence (which was refused), to protect herself from nudists who, she claimed, were exhibiting themselves and causing a nuisance near her property. Council inspectors make occasional raids to arrest offenders for indecent exposure. The Beach was also known as 'Pirates Camp' after a camp of shacks that were built during the depression of the 1930's.

The harbourside beaches on Spring Cove (above) are some of the most pleasant and secluded on the Harbour. In the background the ocean beaches of Manly and the Northern Beaches stretch to the horizon.

A yacht gently tacks around Cannae Point (above) at Manly Quarantine Station. A warning flag was raised on the flagpole on the point if passengers carrying infectious disease were in residence.

A small craft (right) approaches the wharf at the Quarantine Station. The movie 'A Town Like Alice' was filmed on location in the old buildings of the Station.

Dobroyd Head

The walk continues on the main track uphill through the heathland of Dobroyd Head to Tania Park, named after local Manly girl Tania Verstak, crowned 'Miss Australia' in 1961 and 'Miss International Beauty' in 1962. At the north east corner of the park Arabanoo Lookout offers a superb vista of the Harbour, Manly Peninsular and the Pacific Ocean. The lookout is named after the Aborigine Arabanoo, the first aborigine to be captured by the marines from Manly in December 1788 and taken back to Sydney. He lived for a time with Phillip as his helper, assisting in the treatment of aborigines who'd caught smallpox, before succumbing to the disease himself. He was buried in the grounds of Government House in May 1789.

Not far from Arabanoo Lookout on the east side of Dobroyd Head Scenic Drive, a track overlooks the settlement of Crater Valley, perched on the heights of Dobroyd Head above Crater Cove. Still standing on the north side of the headland are several inhabited huts, that originated as squatters huts during the

Pleasure craft off Store Beach on a summer weekend (above). The Beach was named after the 'stores' that were unloaded there for the Quarantine Station.

Little Manly Cove (foreground below) has the closest boat launching ramp to Manly. The park on Little Manly Point next to the beach is constructed on the site of a former gasworks. Secluded Collins Beach in the background is accessible only by bush track or by boat.

A ferry approaches the wharf at Manly (previous pages). First time visitors to Manly can be disorientated to discover beaches on both sides of the town. The small sandy strip of Delwood Beach can just be picked out in the shadow of the pine trees near the blocks of apartments at the lower left of the picture.

The harbourside pool at Fairlight Beach (above). Skirting the shore below the houses and apartments is a section of the walking track leading from Manly Cove to North Harbour Reserve.

depression of the 1920's and have remained ever since. At that time Dobroyd Head was army property and some of the squatters had the permission of the army to stay there. Whole families used to live in the huts like pioneers, with no gas, electricity or running water. They built a rock swimming pool in the bay below

and cleared small patches for growing vegetables. One of the early 'official' residents, Fred Williams, who built a shack here in 1929, died at the "Crater" fighting a bushfire. A plaque close to the spot where he died reads "In memory of Fredk. Chas. Williams, Honorary Ranger, who died here 28th April 1940." The waters off Crater Cove are the site of Gowland Bombora, which is dangerous for small craft particularly when a heavy swell is coming through the heads. A bombora is an unpredictable surge of water passing over a shallow rock formation. The navigator Commander John Gowland R.N. (who rescued Eliza Frazer from the island in Queensland which now bears her name) drowned here while surveying Middle Harbour in 1874.

Continuing on the walking track through a landscape of open heathland, you soon reach another lookout on the rocks close to the end of Cutler Road Balgowlah Heights. The view from here of Middle Harbour,

Forty Baskets Beach (left).

Dobroyd Head (right), with the waters of Middle Harbour in the background. A scenic drive skirts the green patch of Tania Park at the top of the headland. 'Crater Valley' is just to the left of the park, 'Washaway Beach' is on the nearside of the point at far left and 'Reef Beach' on the lower right.

Nude bathers at sheltered Reef Beach (below) had to once hastily don their clothes to be evacuated when a bushfire raged across Dobroyd Head.

the sweep of Balmoral Beach and North and South Head, is particularly rewarding on a fine weekend when the white sails of numerous boats dot the Harbour.

Grotto Point

A fork off the main track leads to Grotto Point Lighthouse. The Point was named by a survey party from the First Fleet who camped here on 28th January 1788 after the caves or 'grottoes' in the sandstone rocks above nearby Castle Rock Beach. The lighthouse, built in 1911, guides ships entering Sydney Harbour when aligned with the Pirriwi light on Cremorne Point.

Not far from the lighthouse on the east side of the Point is Washaway Beach, whose sands ebb and flow according to the level of storm activity. On the rocks above the beach are some aboriginal carvings including a fish, an emu and a kangaroo, though the kangaroo is generally considered to be the work of 'white fellas'.

MIDDLE HARBOUR

Rugged bushwalks and beautiful harbour beaches

Finish the walk to The Spit and see aboriginal sites in the untamed bushland of Bantry Bay and Davidson Park. Harbourside walks skirt the headlands of eastern Middle Harbour through a rocky terrain sheltered by a variety of native forest. Finally see the beaches on the south shore of Middle Harbour including the Queen of Sydney's harbour beaches, Balmoral.

———————————————

Continuing on the walk to The Spit from Grotto Point, the track heads east into Middle Harbour past a long flight of steps that lead down to the small sandy cove of Castle Rock Beach, then through some dense heath and woodland below tall sandstone rock formations to enter Duke of Edinburgh Reserve. From the reserve it's about another ten minutes walk through a short stretch of bushland and across Clontarf Beach to the picnic ground of Clontarf, named after a resort on the Bay of Dublin. The reserve is on an old Aboriginal Corroboree ground called 'Warringa' after which the Shire of Warringah is named.

Clontarf

On the 12 March 1868 the 23 year old son of Queen Victoria, Prince Alfred the Duke of Edinburgh was the guest of honour at a formal picnic at Clontarf while visiting Australia during a world tour on board the warship *HMS Galatea* when he was shot by an Irish supporter of the anti-royalist Fennian society, Henry O'Farrell. The Prince staggered and fell crying 'Good God I am shot, my back is broken.' By a stroke of luck the force of the bullet was partly absorbed by the Prince's india-rubber braces. Operated on a few days later at Government House Sydney, with two nurses in attendance trained by

Florence Nightingale, the Prince made a full recovery and continued with his world tour. O'Farrell was hanged for his trouble at Darlinghurst Gaol on 21st of April that year.

From Clontarf the walk continues around Sandy Bay, where a broad sand flat is exposed at low tide, around the lookout of Fisher Point on top of which is the protected archaeological site of an aboriginal shell midden, to Fisher Bay. Above the Bay is a particularly pleasant stretch of the walk through a pocket of sub-tropical rainforest. On one section the track crosses the water at the head of the Bay on a wooden boardwalk beneath a cool overhanging rock shelf where ferns and other plants spring from indentations in the rock.

The Spit

After climbing up a flight of stone steps from Fisher Bay, the track follows a gently graded broad path for two hundred metres along the route of the old tram line from Manly to The Spit. The track finishes at a small reserve and parking area next to the Spit Bridge.

The Spit Bridge is named after the sand spit that extends from the south shore of Middle Harbour. For no less

The Captain Cook cruise boat ventures up Middle Harbour on a sightseeing tour (previous pages at lower right of picture).

The calm waters of Middle Harbour look dramatically different on an overcast day (below). Grotto Point lighthouse can just be picked out at the end of the Point at the lower centre of the picture. Washaway Beach is nearby on the lower right.

The sandy beach at Clontarf Reserve (above). Sandy Bay at the top of the picture becomes completely covered at high tide.

than 38 years, from 1850 to 1888 Peter Ellery ran a hand punt service across the narrow channel of Middle Harbour from the end of the sand spit to the present site of the reserve on the north shore next to the Spit Bridge. In those days 'Jenkins Road', the first road to Manly, ran from the north side of Middle Harbour to the present site of North Harbour Reserve. A government steam punt provided a service on the crossing from 1889 to 1924 when the first toll bridge opened. In its last year of operation, the punt carried 300,000 motor vehicles, 20,000 cycles and 50,000 horse drawn vehicles. The remains of the stone landing ramp for the punt

can be seen in the reserve next to the Spit. The present Spit Bridge with its single lift span was opened in 1958. It's span lifts 8 times a day during the week and thirteen times a day at weekends to allow passage for yachts and ferries up Middle Harbour. The consequent delays are a source of never ending frustration for motorists travelling to and from the northern suburbs to the city. The bridge operator can be contacted to arrange special opening times - though he won't do it just for fun!

Seaforth

Seaforth on the west side of the Spit Bridge was named after Loch Seaforth in Scotland. The first land lots at Seaforth were sold by a gentleman going by the name of Henry Halloran in November 1906. In sympathy with his own name, Halloran

called most of the street names on his estate by the first two letters, including Richmond Road, Princess Promenade, Edgecliff Esplanade, Alan Avenue, Ponsonbury Parade and Battle Boulevard. Lots of land on Seaforth Bluff on the west side of Seaforth headland were sold by auction from the deck of the steamer *Lady Rawson*, which halted opposite each block as it was offered for sale while prospective buyers were kept in the right mood by a band playing on deck.

The quietness of this reach of the Harbour in the nineteenth century made it a safe place to keep gunpowder moored on ship's hulks in "Powder Hulk Bay". From the 1870's to the turn of the century hulks such as the *Pride of England* and an ex-American ship, the *Behring*, launched originally in 1850, were anchored in

Traffic banks up on both sides of the Spit Bridge (above) as it's single span is raised to allow passage for ferries and yachts on Middle Harbour.

the Bay. The Behring was eventually towed to Sailors Bay and burnt to the waterline. At low tide the remains of it's hull can be seen on the mudflats near Sailors Bay Park.

Bantry Bay

Bantry Bay north of Seaforth remains a remote, thickly wooded corner of Middle Harbour. It's an area particularly rich in aboriginal history, with many tool sharpening grooves near creek beds and rock shelters where the Aborigines once lived and hunt-

The Roseville Bridge carries traffic on Warringah Road over the upper reaches of Middle Harbour (above).

Disused explosives magazines on Bantry Bay (below).

Houses are scattered among the bushland on the steep headland of Castlecrag (above right).

Sugarloaf Bay (above right) separates the suburbs of Castle Cove left and Castlecrag right. Harold Reid Reserve on Middle Cove is at lower right. There have been five fatal shark attacks in Middle Harbour in relatively recent times, all outside netted areas; two in 1942, two in 1955 and the last in

1963, when a young actress Marcia Hathaway was killed swimming at Sugarloaf Bay.

ed. A particularly significant set of aboriginal carvings has been etched onto some flat rocks close to a footpath at the end of Bantry Bay Road, where there are eighty or more figures including wallabies, a dingoe, an echidna, snakes, whales and fish, boomerangs, axes and clubs, and a bark canoe and shield. Sadly, many of these carvings have now been all but obliterated by the elements.

A good walk in the area lasting about two and a half hours starts from the end of Bantry Bay Road in Frenchs Forest. The suburb is named after James French, a settler who ran a woodcutting enterprise from his landholding in the area acquired in

1856. Using manual labour the great gum trees were cut down, split with steel wedges and hammers, then hauled by bullocks along Bantry Bay Road and down to a wharf (which still exists) on the south east side of the bay. Leaving your car, walk to the end of Utyana Place and turn left across a patch of grass before the scout hall to a track through the bush, which leads after five or ten minutes walk to a rocky bluff with a beautiful view of Bantry Bay, Middle Harbour and the distant city skyline. Scrambling down some rocks from the top of the bluff, the track drops steeply to the east shore of Bantry Bay, then follows the shoreline through the woods just above the Bay to reach after forty minutes or so a grassy area with two or three terraces running up the hillside. Here there are toilets, fresh water and barbecue places. In the 1890's Thomas Walters lived in a house here with his wife and children. They kept goats on the other side of the bay, fished in the waters of Middle Harbour, and made honey

from beehives they kept near the house. An Irishman, John Dunbar Nelson, built a dance hall near the Walters home, and ran pleasure steamers carrying picnic parties on Sundays to the site. Dunbar boasted in his advertisements that Bantry Bay had 'Swings and Merry-go-rounds, Summer Houses and shady nooks, also Dancing and Dining Pavilions, (in scenery which) may be classed the "Killarney of Australia"'. Thomas Walters was caretaker of the dance hall, and played in the dance band. After the picnic grounds were closed on the opening of the explosives depot on the west side of the bay in 1915, two of the Walters children found jobs there. When the suburb of Killarney Heights overlooking the other side of the Bay was developed in the early twentieth century, many of the streets were named after places in Ireland, including, Tipperary Avenue, Londonderry Drive, Bally-shannon Road and Dublin Avenue.

Below the old picnic grounds are the remains of a coal loading jetty

used to refuel ships using the explosives depot during the First World War, and a small boat slipway. Continue past these along the shore to a point where the track branches off into the bush. On this section the track is following the route of the old timber-getters trail, and you soon pass a wall of sandstone blocks next to a creek bed that once supported a log bridge for the trail. The track continues climbing through the bush to come out after 15 minutes at Seaforth Oval. Turn left on the nearby Wakehurst Parkway and walk for three hundred metres to a stone memorial celebrating the opening of the Parkway, just behind which is the access to the 'Engravings Track' following the route of French's old bullock trail. Notice the many deep scratches on exposed rocks along the trail caused by the axles of bullock carts dragging over them. On the left, shortly before the track joins Bantry Bay Road, are the aboriginal rock 'engravings', cordoned off by a chain fence.

The Magazine Track

On the east side of the Bay, another walking track heads south from the playing fields at the end of Currie Road Forestville, leading eventually after two hours walk to Roseville Bridge. Fifteen minutes walk from Currie Road an indistinct one-way track marked by a white arrow on a scribbly gum, branches off downhill on the left to an interesting natural rock bridge over Main Creek. Further along, the main trail becomes the 'Magazine Track', which skirts the old explosives depot on the east side of the Bay.

Work started in 1909 on the construction of twelve brick magazines,

set back into cuttings in the rock of the valleyside so that if there was an explosion the force of the blast would be directed upward. Built to replace the old powder hulks in Powder Hulk Bay, the new magazines were constructed on a long stone jetty running parallel to the shoreline with its own tram tracks to facilitate loading and unloading of explosives. The complex was closed in 1974, and though the installations remain substantially intact, they are currently off-limits to the public.

The Magazine Track continues through the bushland, swinging west at the opening of the Bay to Flat Rock, a clearing in the bush above a

small sandy beach. Flat rock was another stopping off point for Nelson's pleasure steamers, which he advertised as 'A perfect place to camp out... without fear of monotony.' Some writing has been chiselled into the rocks, including the names of Nelson's pleasure steamers. Continuing west on the track, after a kilometre you reach Killarney Point. Above what were once well tended lawns you pass the remains of a dance hall and a caretakers lodge, all that's left of Nelson's Killarney Point Picnic Ground. Nelson himself came to live at Killarney Point in 1913 and he and his sons continued to skipper his pleasure steamers until well into the twentieth century. The walking track

continues to a large modern day picnic area below Roseville Bridge, with barbecue places and picnic tables (accessible by road only by the west bound carriageway of Warringah Road). The modern high level Roseville Bridge opened in 1965 to replace an earlier structure first opened in 1924.

Davidson Park

Davidson Park on the north side of the Roseville bridge, covering 1200 hectares, is the largest area of natural bushland remaining on the shores of Sydney Harbour. On his exploration through the district on 16th April 1788, Governor Phillip described the scene near the tidal limit of Middle

Harbour Creek, 'Here in the most deserted, wild and solitary seclusion that the imagination can form any idea of, we took up our abode for the night'. A scene that remains unchanged to this day, as any intrepid bushwalker who has ventured into the upper reaches of Middle Harbour Creek will quickly testify.

The area of the park comprises a series of bush covered valleys cut into the sandstone of the surrounding plateau covered by a great variety of flora, from heathland and open areas of eucalypt forest, to groves of palm trees, jungle like environments with creepers hanging off the trees and shaded gullies with moss and ferns coating the rocks and tree trunks.

The fortress like Cammeray Bridge dating to the 1880's (above left) had the longest concrete arch span in the southern hemisphere when it was converted from a suspension bridge during the 1930's.

Long Bay (above) with the suburbs of Northbridge on the left and Spit Junction and Beauty Point on the right. In the foreground Northbridge Golf Course is on the left and Primrose Park on Willoughby Bay on the right.

Three house-boats on Pearl Bay (above) can just be seen at the bottom of the picture. In the foreground on the right are the Spit Reserve and the seldom visited bushland of Parriwi Park.

Chinamans Beach and Rosherville Reserve (above right).

Yachts berthed at the marinas of Middle Harbour Yacht Club (below).

There are many rewarding bushwalks through the park, too numerous to mention here, however it is worth describing the route of two of the best. The first, a walk of two hours, starts on Eastern Arterial Road in East Lindfield near Gordon Creek and finishes at Babbage Road just south of the Roseville Bridge. The second a walk of five hours, leads off Stone Parade near the junction of Barney Place in Frenchs Forest, to a small waterfall at 'The Cascades', then follows Middle Harbour Creek downstream through Phillip's 'deserted, wild and solitary seclusion' to a pipeline over the creek. Turn left on a track to follow the pipeline up to Prahran Avenue Davidson, from where it's a 40 minute walk through the streets to return to Stone Parade.

Castle Cove

South of the Roseville Bridge opposite Killarney Heights is the peninsula of Castle Cove. Between 1903 and 1905 Henry Hastings Willis, an MP in the first Federal Parliament of 1901,

built 'Innisfallen Castle' on a magnificent site on the southern side of Castle Cove with beautiful views of Middle Harbour and the surrounding headlands. Standing today at 14 Cherry Place off Willis Road, the house, named after Innisfallen Castle in Ireland, was originally surrounded by 21 hectares of virgin bushland and was accessible only by a bullock track or by water. Built like a castle, with stone walls, ramparts and a tower, the house had staff quarters, a ballroom, dining room, large reception room and eight marble fireplaces for heating. Willis ran the property as if at any time he expected to withstand a siege; a governess, cook, housemaids and farmhands lived in the staff quarters, while corn, oats, potatoes and salted eggs were stored in the basement. The children of the household travelled to school by boat after descending a steep track to Sugarloaf Bay.

A three hour bushwalk from the end of Cammaray Road in Castle Cove, follows the harbour shore to the Harold Reid Reserve on Middle Cove. The walk starts at HC Press Park, named after the entrepreneur H.C. Press, who transformed 6 hectares of land he owned at the tip of Castle Cove into 'picnic grounds' in the 1870's. Every Sunday ferries and boats brought parties of daytrippers, often comprised of complete family groups of thirty or more including nannies, cooks, and butlers. In the southern section of the park are the remains of the dance hall, a landing jetty, steps, paths, seats and terraces that testify to the park's heyday. When the picnic grounds closed, H.C. Press built his own house nearby at Castle Cove.

Middle Cove

The bush track winds above the shore of Castle Cove to Scotts Creek, then skirts the perimeter of Middle Cove to finish at 114 Sugarloaf Crescent. The Peninsula of Middle Cove is covered by a park of virgin bushland called the 'Harold Reid Reserve', named after the Town Clerk of Willoughby in 1963. A narrow one way road encir-

cling the crown of the headland leads to several clearings in the woods, with picnic tables and superb views through the trees of Middle Harbour. The steeply sloping headland is also known as 'The Sugarloaf'. At the time of the pioneers, refined sugar was pressed into conical shaped "loaves".

Castle Crag

The suburb of Castle Crag south of Middle Cove was named after a large rocky outcrop on the peak of the headland that was identified on early maps as 'Edinburgh Castle'. Edinburgh Road that runs from High Street Willoughby across the crown of the headland is named after it.

The layout of the streets today in Castlecrag is the work of the American architect Walter Burley Griffin, a colleague of Frank Lloyd Wright, who arrived in Australia in 1913 to supervise the design for Canberra, which he had won the international competition for in 1912. Following endless disagreements with the Government

Balmoral Beach (left) with Sydney Harbour and the City in the background.

Cobblers Beach (right) is accessible after a ten minute walk through Middle Head Oval, past the army barracks and along a winding track through the bush.

Balmoral Beach with the extensive bushland of Georges Heights and Middle Head on the right (below). On the far side of the Sound are Dobroyd on the left and Manly and North Head in the distance on the right.

over the Canberra project, Griffin resigned, moved to Sydney, and with the financial backing of a group of Melbourne businessman embarked on an ambitious project to develop housing in the uninhabited bushland of Castlecrag. The streets, curved to follow the natural terraces of the steep rocky slopes of the suburb, were given the names of parts of a medieval castle, such as The Tor Walk, The Barbette, The Parapet, The Rampart, The Redoubt and so on. However the avant garde houses, built in Griffin's own particular style with flat roofs, kitchens at the front and no fences, were hard to sell during the depression, and only a handful were built of the scores that had been planned. Griffin lived at Castle Crag for twelve years before moving to India with his wife to work on the design of a library at Lucknow University, a building which incidentally he referred to as

an Opera House for Sydney". Griffin passed away aged 61 the year after he arrived in India.

Griffins own house he built in 1922 still exists today at number 8 The Parapet. Other houses he designed include 14 The Parapet, and numbers 2 ,4 and 8 The Barbette. An open air theatre called the New Haven where the Griffins cajoled their neighbours into braving the mosquitoes at night to perform in Greek dramas under the light of magnesium flares, still remains today in the reserve at the junction of The Scarp and The Barricade.

Northbridge

The harbourside suburb of Northbridge takes it's name from Cammeray Bridge (itself named after the Cammaraygal Aboriginal tribe who used to inhabit much of the North Shore). The Bridge, an extra-ordinary structure with twin sets of

battlemented towers, was designed by New Zealand Architect, D.Ross. Originally a suspension bridge built by the North Sydney Tramway and Development Company to help sell real estate on the far side of Salt Pan Cove, construction commenced in 1889, but the cost of the Bridge sent the Development Company bankrupt. Construction was taken over by the Government, who completed the Bridge in 1892, charging a 1d toll on vehicles to recoup their costs. The original suspension bridge was condemned in 1936, and the present reinforced concrete bridge retaining the original battlemented towers was opened in 1939. At the time of its construction the bridge had the longest concrete arch span in the southern hemisphere.

Beauty Point across the water from Northbridge, was originally called Billy Goat Point, then renamed Beauty Point by a real estate developer called Fitzpatrick who was selling building blocks in the 1920's. Beautiful it may have been, but there were no buyers for his land during the depression and he went bankrupt.

Pearl Bay

Floating on nearby Pearl Bay are three house boats, the legacy of a much larger fleet which were moored on the Bay during the depression as a cheap form of housing. The houseboats that exist today were originally officially registered early in the twentieth century and despite protracted legal battles to try to outlaw them, they have been grudgingly accepted and are now part of the scenery. Some are literally like floating houses, large

Before Balmoral Beach was named after Queen Victoria's Scottish estate the beach was known as Hunters Bay after Captain John Hunter of the First Fleet ship the 'Sirius'. Hunter later became Governor of New South Wales.

and comfortable and well decorated inside, one even has a garden on the roof. When they change hands they fetch the same price as a medium size house. One of the houseboats is built on the platform of the punt that used to run across the Spit.

A one and a half kilometre bush track follows the Harbour shoreline from The Spit Reserve (created during the 1960's with sandstone landfill from the cutting for the six lane Spit Road to the Spit Bridge), past the house-boats resting gently at their moorings to Pulpit Rock at Quakers Hat on the west side of Beauty Point. Some of the streets of Beauty Point are named after the battle grounds where Australians fought during the First World War, such as Amiens and Bullecourt Avenues, others have strange names like Medusa Street, and Ida and Delecta Avenues.

Chinamans Beach

At low tide a fifteen minute walk leads from Middle Harbour Yacht Club at the Spit across the sandy beach at Parriwi Head and the rocks of Shell Cove to Chinamans Beach.

Chinamans Beach, with its neighbouring Rosherville Reserve, rivals Clontarf on the opposite side of Middle Harbour as one of the best places on Sydney Harbour for a barbecue and swim on a summer evening. The Beach was named after Chinese market gardens which existed in the nineteenth century on the flat ground of present day Rosherville Reserve.

Balmoral

Balmoral, south of Chinamans Beach, is named after the Royal Family's estate in Scotland built by Queen Victoria in 1853. The bay is really two beaches, Edwards at the north and Balmoral at the south, separated by a tiny isthmus leading to the equally diminutive grassy knoll of Rocky Point. The point becomes an island at high tide, joined to the promenade at Balmoral by a concrete footbridge.

Edwards Beach was named after an early resident, Captain Edwards, who had a house near the present day site of the band rotunda. If he stirs in his grave at the thought his house was knocked down, at least he can console himself in the knowledge that 'Shakespeare by the Sea' is performed in the rotunda on summer evenings.

During the 1880's semi-permanent camps of tents and shacks were built on the flat ground behind Balmoral Beach by "bohemians" and artists or single men working in Sydney who could afford nowhere else to stay. Forced to conform to local bye-laws in 1907, by 1921 the camps had disappeared altogether.

On the heights at the northern end of Edwards beach a red brick block of flats stands on the site of an earlier building that was built in one of Sydney's weirder moments . In 1923 a Romanesque amphitheatre was constructed facing the water in the mistaken belief that a Messiah was going to walk through the Heads and meet his true believers here. Although seats could be leased for up to 25 years, no Messiah ever crossed the bay on foot. The amphitheatre, built by the theosophists of the Order of the Star of the East, was demolished in 1939.

Cobblers Beach

On the eastern heights above Balmoral, the naval base of HMAS Penguin has the Royal Australian Naval Hospital in the grounds. The last beach on Middle Harbour, Cobblers Beach, directly opposite Grotto Point, is accessible by boat or after a quarter of an hours walk from Middle Head Oval. It is one of Sydney's unofficial nudist beaches.

———————————

MIDDLE HEAD TO MILSONS POINT

Harbour fortifications and Taronga Zoo

See the network of old harbour defences at Middle Head, Georges Head and Bradleys Head. Visit one of the most beautiful zoo sites in the world and explore the streets and parks of the North Shore suburbs of Mosman, Cremorne, Neutral Bay and Kirribilli.

Middle Head Fort

Middle Head and neighbouring Georges Heights are riddled with a whole network of lookouts, passages, tunnels, stairways and ammunition stores, mostly created in two feverish bursts of activity during the 'Russian Scare' of 1871 and at the start of the Second World War. In the 1860's Russian warships were taking more than a casual interest in Australian ports during long distance 'training expeditions' and the creation of an effective defence for Sydney during the Second World War was spurred on by the Japanese midget sub attack on Sydney Harbour.

The best way to see the old fortifications, is to park at the car park near the corner of Chowder Bay Road and Middle Head Road, walk through Middle Head Oval and behind the army barracks, cross a patch of rough ground to a well preserved weatherboard cottage, then take the straight road that runs directly onto the headland. Besides the relics of the fort on the centre of the headland, there are other tunnels and lookouts close to the shore between Middle Head and Cobblers Beach. The guns of the fort were

never fired in anger, but four men were killed on 4 April 1891 when a mine accidentally exploded. The National Parks and Wildlife Service organise guided tours during school holidays.

Obelisk Bay

From the weatherboard cottage, another track circles south around an army storage depot to return to the car park on Chowder Bay Road. Near the car park a track leads down to Obelisk Bay, yet another of Sydney's unofficial beaches for nudists - or for perverts, depending on your point of view. Above the rocks between Obelisk Bay and Georges Head are more gun emplacements, lookouts and tunnels, many still in a reasonable state of preservation, even with the wooden joinery still in place sometimes when the vandals haven't got to them. Georges Head was first made the site of a battery by Governor King in 1801. All the fortifications in the area are preserved as structures of historical interest.

Georges Heights, named after George III, was known as 'King Bungaree's Farm' for a time after Macquarie tried to resettle sixteen aboriginal families here including the last chief of the Cammaraygals King Bungaree and his wife 'Queen Gooseberry'. The King had earlier sailed with Matthew Flinders on his epic map-making circumnavigation of Australia in 1802-03.

Clifton Gardens

The sandy beach at Chowder Bay is accessible from Morella Road Clifton Gardens. American whaling ships used to anchor in the bay and make clam 'chowder' from oysters they collected off the rocks. Chowder is a seafood soup famous on the American east coast. The skipper of one of the whaling ships, Captain Cliffe of the *Lady Wellington*, bought land in the locality in 1832 and built a house overlooking the bay called 'Cliffeton', with the result that the suburb subsequently became known as Clifton Gardens. The flat land close to the beach was perfect for a park, and later owners built the three storey Marine Hotel and operated picnic and pleasure grounds, bringing revellers from Sydney by ferry. When the park was bought out by Sydney Ferries in 1906, they built a dance hall in the park, a large circular swimming pool in the bay, renamed the Marine Hotel the Clifton Gardens Hotel, and advertised the spot as the 'biggest pleasure grounds in the Southern Hemisphere'. These days the pleasure grounds are nothing but a memory. The circular swimming pool no longer exists and even the Clifton Gardens Hotel was bought by Mosman Council in 1969 and demolished. Modern day visitors to Clifton Gardens must find their own entertainment at the grassy reserve or on the beach.

Previous pages: The liner 'QE 2' berths at Sydney Cove Passenger Terminal as 'The Russ' passes beneath Sydney Harbour Bridge. Milsons Point is on the far side of the bridge.

Middle Head commands the south side of the entrance to Middle Harbour (far left).

The old gun emplacements, stores and tunnels at Middle Head Fort (left) are now a protected historical site open to the public as part of Sydney Harbour

Clifton Gardens Reserve on Chowder Bay (far right).

Quiet Obelisk Bay (right) is named after two white obelisks in the bush above the bay that are used as navigation markers by ships entering the harbour.

A World War Two lookout and gun emplacement on Georges Head (right).

Three cannon on carriages at the top of Bradleys Head (right) date to the 1870's.

600 tonne coastal steamer the *Centennial*. On 23 August 1889 the *Centennial* was rounding Bradleys Head outward bound from Sydney, when it struck the inward bound collier *Kanahooka*. All the eighty passengers and crew from the *Centennial* were rescued, except for the chief cook, who was drowned when the ship went down.

On this section of the walk, is a particularly attractive sheltered spot at the head of Taylors Bay, where a small stream cascades over rocks, surrounded by lush vegetation including cabbage tree palms and tree ferns.

Bradleys Head

From Taylors Bay it's a further half an hours walk to Bradleys Head, named after Lieutenant William Bradley, First Lieutenant of *HMS Sirius* and a cartographer with the First Fleet. Bradley enjoyed a distinguished career in the Royal Navy following his sojourn in New South Wales, retiring as a Rear Admiral of the Blue in 1812. However in 1814 he was convicted of fraud at Winchester assizes and sentenced to death. The punishment was commuted to transportation for life, but before the sentence could be carried out, Bradley escaped to France and lived there for the rest of his life.

Three cannon in gun pits on the top of Bradleys Head are the best remaining examples of a series of fortifications that were built on harbour headlands in the 1840's and 1870's. Above some more old fortifications on the south side of the head, stands the mast and crows nest of the First World War battle cruiser *HMAS Sydney*. On September 9 1914 the *Sydney* was on convoy escort duty when it intercepted a message from the wireless station on the Cocos Islands that it was under attack by a raiding party from the *Emden*. At the time the *Emden* was the scourge of the Indian Ocean and although the war was only a few weeks old, she had

A walk to the Zoo

From Clifton Gardens a two hour walk on a bush track follows the harbour shoreline to Taronga Zoo. The track starts above the beach at Clifton Gardens Reserve, then climbs through the bush to Chowder Head. A short deviation is well worthwhile here to a lookout at the tip of the head with beautiful views of Sydney Harbour. The walk continues east to Taylors Bay, named after James Taylor of Macquarie's 73rd Regiment of Highlanders who arrived in Sydney in 1810. Towering above the bay on Iluka Road is one of the biggest houses in Sydney, 'The Manor', built by David Thomson,

owner of the Marine Hotel and the Clifton estate from 1891 to 1906. A later owner of the house were the Theosophists who built the amphitheatre at Balmoral. Their guru, Krishnamurti, stayed there when he was in Sydney to 'perform' at the amphitheatre. The house was the first broadcasting studio of well-known Sydney radio station 2GB, "GB" being the initials of Giordano Bruno, an Italian Dominican monk burned at the stake for heresy in 1600 who inspired the Theosophists and the radio station with his ideals of free speech.

On the seabed of Taylors Bay in 16 fathoms of water lies the wreck of the

Summer afternoon storm clouds gather over the City (top) in this view photographed from the park at Bradleys Head.

The French frigate 'Amiral Charner' (above) entering the harbour off Bradleys Head during celebrations for the Bicentennial Navy Salute in 1988.

already seized or sunk 23 merchant ships, 2 warships and had shelled Madras. The Sydney steamed directly for the Cocos Islands and immediately engaged the enemy. Following a brief ferocious battle the *Emden*, outgunned by the faster and heavier Australian ship was left beached and holed on the rocks of the island. One

hundred and ten prisoners were taken from the *Emden* including the Captain, however the shore party who had raided the radio station escaped in a stolen cutter and after many adventures eventually returned to Germany via Arabia and Turkey. The mast of the cruiser stands as a memorial to the four men of the

Sydney killed in the action. Another memorial close by pays tribute to the second *Sydney*, which was sunk with all hands off the coast of West Australia during a battle with the German raider *Kormoran* in 1942.

On the rocks below the mast of the Sydney, is a pillar from the portico of the old Sydney GPO building, demolished in 1875. Between 1875 and 1912, ships built in Sydney carrying out their sea trials ran speed tests on the 'measured mile' from Fort Denison on the Harbour to the pillar at Bradleys Head. The practice was halted because of the danger to other shipping.

Continue on the bush track, as it

The mast of the First World War cruiser the 'Sydney' on Bradleys Head (above). The old stone wharf on the left, now a popular fishing spot, was used to unload stores for the fort on the Head.

follows the shore through unspoilt bushland with glimpses through the trees across the Harbour to the city and Opera House. After fifteen minutes you pass a flat grassy area on the right with swings and an old hall. This is Athol Hall, the only survivor of the many dancing halls that were once scattered along the Harbour shores, serviced by ferries. After a further five minutes walk you reach the south entrance of Taronga Zoo. The wharf next to the Zoo was once a terminus for tram services from Mosman. On no less than three occasions the tram failed to stop and plunged into the Harbour, fortunately with no injury, other than hurt pride.

Taronga Zoo

The original Sydney Zoo was founded on three hectares of land on the other side of the Harbour by the Zoological Society of New South Wales in 1881 on a site known as 'Billygoat Swamp' at Moore Park. When the Zoo outgrew that site, twelve hectares were made available in 1912 at the present location for a new Zoo. All the animals were transported across the Harbour to their new home on vehicle ferries, including Jessie the elephant, an old favourite of Moore Park, who was a gift from the King of Siam in 1883. She lived happily at her new home until passing away in 1938.

From close to the wharf a cable car offers a two-minute ride over the hippos and alligators to the top entrance to Taronga Zoo. Taronga is aboriginal for beautiful view and I think that without question, everyone would agree, that Taronga Zoo, on its site overlooking Sydney Harbour, is the most beautiful zoo location in the world. A map of the Zoo is available at the shop near the entrance to guide you to the location of Australia's unique wildlife, including koalas, kangaroos, emus, wombats and that extraordinary legacy of the dinosaur age, the duck-billed platypus. There's also an impressive array of creatures from other parts of the world, including rhinos, big cats, apes and bears. Don't miss the entertaining squirrel monkeys and otters.

Little Sirius Cove

A harbourside track leads from Taronga Park Wharf, around Whiting Beach and Little Sirius Point to the park at Sirius Cove Reserve. The Cove is named after the Sirius, flagship of the First Fleet, which was 'careened' around the corner at Great Sirius Cove (now known as Mosman Bay) in 1789. Careened means to lay a ship on her side to scrape the hull free of marine growth. The Sirius had just come back from Cape Town with supplies, returning to Sydney via Cape Horn and skirting Antarctica to take advantage of the 'roaring forties'. She was the first ship to circumnavigate the globe in those latitudes. Francis Hill, a masters mate from the Sirius, left Careening Cove near Kirribilli to walk overland to Great Sirius Cove to rejoin his ship, but never made it. He disappeared in the bush and is assumed to have been killed by aborigines.

At the end of the nineteenth century the area around Little Sirius Cove was still secluded bushland. A semi-permanent camp of pioneer style huts and shacks sprang up around the Cove, inhabited by writers and artists who took comfort in the peaceful surroundings and solitude. Painters of the 'Heidelberg School' such as Arthur Streeton, Tom Roberts and Julian Ashton lived here at various times. Some of Tom Roberts' well known works of Sydney Harbour were painted while he resided here, including 'Curlew Camp', a view of the camp painted from near Little Sirius Point. As development encroached on the area the inhabitants of the camp moved away, sometimes to other sqatters camps such as Balmoral,

until by about 1910 it had been abandoned altogether.

At the west side of the park cross Curlew Camp Road, climb the steps to Illawarra Street and walk through Mosman's residential streets for a kilometre to Mosman Wharf.

Mosman, called Corimbullagong by the Cammaraygal tribe, meaning 'peaceful waters', was the abode of the last member of the tribe, nicknamed Tarpot, who lived in a cave near Mosman Wharf and used to help around the Mosman boatsheds in the 1880's.

In 1828, a Scot, Archibald Mosman arrived in Sydney from the West Indies where he had tried sugar growing, intent on establishing a base in Sydney for the whaling industry. Following fierce opposition to his initial plan to moor ships in Sydney Cove because of the fearful smell of whale blubber stored in ships' holds for several months at sea, he was granted four acres at 'Mosman Bay' on the other side of the harbour. Mosman eventually expanded his land holding to 100 acres, and built a stone wharf, storehouse, accommodation for his whaling crews and a house for himself 'The Nest' on 30 acres surrounded by orchards and grapevines. Mosman had come into the whaling industry at just the right time. There was great demand for whale oil as an industrial lubricant and for oil street lamps, and by 1833, the year that whaling ships started calling at Mosman Bay, exports of whale bone and oil provided over half the export income of New South Wales. Mosman sold his whaling business at the end of the 1830's for a sum that included an annual annuity of £2,000, which he lost when the new company went bankrupt following the depression of the 1840's. The general economic situation wasn't helped by a slackening in world demand for whale oil, which was being replaced in the 1840's by gas in street lighting.

Mosman

In 1859 Mosman's house and land were purchased by an Irishman, Richard Hayes Harnett, 'The Father of Mosman', after whom Harnett Park on the waterfront of the Bay is named. Harnett quarried sandstone from his property which he sold for buildings in Sydney, including the construction of the sea wall around Farm Cove in the Botanic Gardens, started the first ferry service to Mosman in 1871, and in 1874 subdivided part of his land into 45 lots for sale for houses. Five years later in 1879 he established a horse drawn carriage service from Mosman Wharf to Military Road. His son was the first Mayor of Mosman.

Archibald Mosman retired to Coogee where he passed away peacefully in 1863. His grave takes pride of place in the churchyard of St Jude's Church Randwick. His old stone house 'The Nest' was demolished in 1931, however Mosman's stone storehouse near Mosman wharf, nick-

named 'The Old Barn', survived, and is now the Mosman Scout Hall. Mosman Wharf itself, on Avenue Road, stands on wooden piles above Mosman's original stone wharf. Incidentally there are two other Avenue Roads in Sydney but no Road Avenues. Other streets in Mosman are named after members of the heroic first 'ashes' Australian Cricket Team of the late nineteenth century, including Spofforth, Bannerman, Boyle and Murdoch Streets. Archibald Mosman's legacy lives on in the Municipality's coat of arms, which feature a picture of a whale.

Cremorne

The original land owner of Cremorne Point on the west side of Mosman Bay was James Robertson after whom Robertson Point at the tip of Cremorne Point is named. Robertson arrived in Sydney in 1822 with his wife and six children and became 'watchmaker' to Governor Brisbane. As a reward for setting up the scientific instruments in

Plumes of spray from the hoses of two fire-fighting tugs make a spectacular welcome for the battleship U.S.S. New Jersey as she enters Sydney for the Bicentennial Navy Salute in 1988. The picture was photographed from Bradleys Head.

Brisbane's Parramatta astronomical observatory, (the first in Australia), Robertson received a reward of a land grant of 35 hectares at Cremorne Point where he built a Georgian style stone house. His son, Sir John Robertson, later five times Premier of New South Wales, used as a lad to tie his clothes to his head, swim from Mrs Macquaries Chair to Fort Denison, where he stopped for a brief rest before continuing to his father's house at Cremorne Point. In 1853 James Robertson sold his house and land to James Milson of Milsons Point, who in turn leased it to two developers, Clarke and Woolcott. They built a pleasure ground on the

The elephants at Taronga Zoo (above) enjoy one of the best views in Sydney.

P & O liners the Pacific Princess (left) and Island Princess (right) make a rare site as they enter the harbour abreast in the picture below. In the background is Bradleys Head and the wharf and buildings of Taronga Zoo.

point with a bandstand, dancing stage and funfair called Cremorne, after Cremorne Gardens in London, transformed Robertson's house into the 'Cremorne Hotel' and brought out pleasure seekers to the park on a ferry service they established from Woolloomooloo. The enterprise collapsed six years after it was founded. When there were moves in 1891 to sub-divide and sell waterfront blocks of land at Cremorne for housing, the Government stepped in and legislation was passed following a subsequent court case that all land from high water mark to 30 metres inland around Cremorne Point was reserved as public property.

In 1893 the first test drilling for coal in Sydney took place at Cremorne when a diamond-drill bore struck a ten foot coal seam at a depth of 2,917 feet. The site is marked with a plaque on the south side of Hodgson Avenue near Kareela Road. The Sydney and Port Hacking Coal Company intended to mine the seam from a pithead at Little Sirius Cove, and tendered a plan with an area for miners' cottages, a reservoir and a forty metre smoke stack. A determined effort by local residents prevented the company from going ahead with the project.

A harbourside track follows the government reserve around Cremorne Point created in 1891, from the end of Harnett Street on Mosman Bay around the peninsular to Bogota Avenue at the head of Shell Cove. It's a simple matter to cross the crown of the point by continuing to the end of Bogota Avenue, crossing Milson Road to Hodgson Avenue directly opposite, and walking to the end to rejoin the path to Harnett Street. There are superb views of the Opera House and city skyline from the picturesque little park on Robertsons Point and from the path on the west side of Cremorne Point. There's even a small well maintained free public swimming pool on the west side of

The crumbling stone wharf to the right of Athol Beach (above) was once used by ferries to bring revellers to the Athol Dance Hall located in the clearing above the Beach. In the middle distance on the left is the red roof of one of Sydney's biggest houses 'The Manor', while behind it on the right Manly Jetcat leaves a white wash on the harbour as it races on its way to Manly.

Whiting Beach (below) is three minutes from Taronga Zoo Wharf on the walk from the south entrance of the Zoo to Little Sirius Cove.

the point at MacCallum Pool to cool off in on a hot day.

Shell Cove was originally called Hungry Bay after two convicts were recaptured there, tired and hungry, after escaping from Pinchgut (Fort Denison) where they'd been marooned on rations of bread and water. The bay was renamed Shell Cove for the shells that were collected around the bay by convict women to burn in lime kilns for brick mortar.

Kurraba Point

Kurraba Point on the west shore of Shell Cove was first known as Thrupps Point after Lieutenant Alfred Thrupp, who arrived in Sydney in 1814 and was assistant Naval Officer under Captain Piper (of Point Piper). He had met Piper's daughter Sarah on the voyage out and they later married and lived at Vaucluse. Thrupp was granted 700 acres on the north side of Neutral Bay, including Kurraba Point but never lived there. In the 1850's a Mr Jarrett built a stone gothic style cottage on the point he called 'Kurraba House'. The house was demolished in 1889. The point also used to be known as ballast point; sailing ships unloading cargo in Sydney would collect rock ballast there if they didn't have a return cargo for their outward bound voyage. A further 8,000 tons of sandstone were quarried from the point for the construction of nearby Fort Denison. The present day park on the south west side of the point was created by North Sydney Council when the Port Jackson Steamship Company moved it's ferry repair workshops from the site to Balmain.

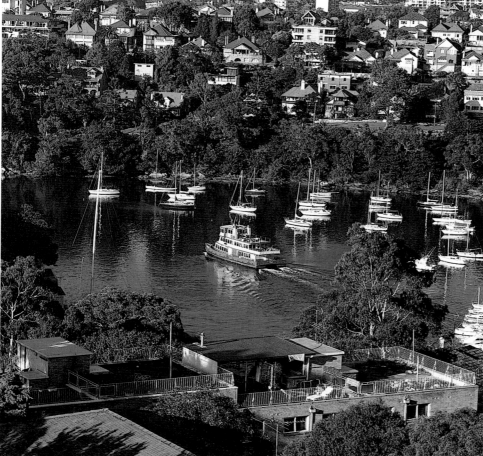

Sirius Park on Little Sirius Cove (above left).

The ferry 'Supply' (left), named after one of the ships of the First Fleet, ripples the waters of tranquil Mosman Bay as it leaves Mosman Wharf for Circular Quay.

Neutral Bay

Nearby Neutral Bay was set aside by Governor Phillip in 1789 as a 'Neutral Bay' where foreign ships were to be moored while visiting Sydney. Crews of the sailing ships used to collect the white sand that then lined the bay 'to scrub the decks of their ships to the peak of perfection'. Ben Boyd Road leading down from Military Road to the bay is named after a Scottish Businessman who founded the 'Bank of Australia' in London, then sailed out to Sydney in his yacht the *Wanderer* to establish a Sydney branch of the bank. Ben Boyd shipped merino wool to Sydney from a large property he owned called 'Boyd Town' on the south coast of New South Wales, to Neutral Bay, where he built a big wool store with a dam for wool washing, fed by fresh water from a creek running down from the nearby heights. When his business empire collapsed in the depression of the 1840's, Boyd lost everything but his yacht, in which he sailed for the Californian goldfields. Not having any luck there, he was on his way back to Australia in the *Wanderer* in 1851 when he was killed and eaten by cannibals while ashore at Guadalcanal in the Solomons bird-shooting. The only trace of him left was his belt which was found by his crew.

Hayes Street Wharf on the site of Boyd's Neutral Bay property was the terminus for trams that ran between Neutral Bay and Military Road via Wycombe Road between 1900 and 1956.

At Anderson Park at the head of the bay, pioneer aviator Charles Kingsford Smith landed his record breaking plane *The Southern Cross* and took off again in 1934 during a voyage around Australia. In 1976 Kingsford Smith's widow, who had re-married and was living in America, was flown back to Sydney for the opening of an estate of town houses on the Bay called Southern Cross Gardens.

HMAS Platypus on the south side of Neutral Bay, occupying an old gas-works site, is the Royal Australian Navy's Sydney submarine base. The black hulls of the submarines moored alongside the quay are an odd sight next to the other yachts and craft moored in the bay. They make an even stranger site scurrying about the harbour waters on manoeuvres, threading their way between the white pleasure craft.

Careening Cove around the point from Neutral Bay was once a sandy bay at the head of the Cove where sailing ships were beached or 'careened' to have their hulls cleaned of marine growth. The land at the head of the Cove has since been reclaimed for Milson Park. James Milson used to grow his vegetables in the vicinity. The Cove was also known in the past as Slaughterhouse Bay after the abattoirs the Milsons operated at the end of Willoughby Street. Sydney's oldest '18 footer' sailing club, the Sydney Flying Squadron, founded in 1890, is on the southern side of the Cove.

Kirribilli

The adjoining suburb of Kirribilli on the western section of the headland takes it's name from kiarabilli, aboriginal for 'place of good fishing'. Admiralty House, on the south east side of the head, stands on one of the most beautiful sites in Sydney, with sweeping views of the harbour and across to the city and Opera House. The land on which the house stands was bought originally in 1806 by Robert Campbell, of Campbell's Stores in the Rocks, who leased it in 1842 to Lieutenant Colonel J.G.N. Gibbs who built a single storey Georgian style house on the site which was completed the following year. In 1856 the Government temporarily took over the house and grounds as an emergency measure to mount cannon in the grounds to protect Sydney in the event of an attack by the Russians during the Crimean War. A later owner of the house was Colonel George Barney, who supervised the construction of Fort Denison. From 1885-1913 the house was lent by the New South Wales Government for use as the official residence of Admirals commanding the British Naval Squadron stationed in Sydney. It's last resident in that capacity, Vice-Admiral Sir George Patey, handed over the house to the Commonwealth Government when he vacated, amid strident protests from the New South Wales Government that the house should have been handed back to them. Following a protracted legal battle, which was finally settled in 1930, the High Court ruled that the house did in fact belong to New South Wales. Admiralty House officially became Commonwealth property in 1945, and is now the Sydney residence of the Governor General of Australia.

Standing just to the north on the point, on what were once part of the grounds of Admiralty House, is Kirribilli House, originally built for a Sydney merchant, Adolf Feez in the 1850's. When a subsequent owner Arthur Allen announced in 1919 that he was going to sub-divide and build on the garden, there was such a public outcry that it was bought by the Australian Government in January 1920 to keep the house and grounds intact. The house is now the Prime Minister's official Sydney Residence, where he occasionally receives visiting dignitaries such as President Bush.

Milsons Point

Milsons Point is named after James Milson, a free settler who arrived in Sydney in 1806 carrying seeds to establish a farm given to him by an acquaintance in England, the botanist Joseph Banks, who had accompanied Captain Cook on his original voyage of discovery to Australia in 1770. Milson was granted 50 acres at Milsons Point by Governor King, land which Milson complained 'was nothing but rocks and stones'. However Milson was assigned convicts to labour on the property, and started in business selling rocks for ballast to ships in Sydney, and rainwater collected from rock pools. Milson built the first house on the north shore of the harbour, 'Milk Cottage' at the present site of the north east harbour Bridge pylon, and eventually established a farm on his property from which he sold dairy products and vegetables to Sydney. Despite various setbacks, such as when Milson and his wife had to be rescued from the point by the sailors from *HMS Warspite* when a fire raged through his property, burning down his house and badly burning his wife, and in May 1814, when a ship, the *Three Bees* caught fire off Milsons Point, setting off the ship's guns, one shot from which landed near Milsons home and the other hitting his boatshed, Milson prospered and became one of the largest land holders in Sydney. He died at his daughter's house Carabella, (Spanish for a basket of flowers), in Milsons Point aged 89 in October 1872. Carabella, a house Milson had built for his daughter, was demolished to make way for a block of flats in 1935, but various stone houses built by Milson and his family still exist in the area, including 54 Willoughby Street, 6 Winslow Street and 'Elamang' and 'Milson House' in the grounds of Loretto Convent on Carrabella Street. Elamang was built in 1851 by James Milson for James Milson junior as a wedding present. Another house called Carabella, built by the mayor and spirit merchant William Tucker, and not connected in any way to the Milson family, has since 1902 been part of the grounds of the Royal Sydney Yacht Squadron on the south shore of Careening Cove. Hanging in the entrance of the old house is the ship's bell from Ben Boyd's yacht the Wanderer. In 1851 when the yacht's crew gave up looking for Ben Boyd on Guadalcanal, they sailed his yacht back to Australia, but were ship-

wrecked at Port Macquarie. The bell was recovered from the wreckage.

Before the construction of the Harbour Bridge, Milsons Point was a bustling vehicle and passenger ferry terminus. Regular steam ferry services between Milsons Point and Circular Quay were started by the North Shore Ferry Company with the launch of the Kirribilli in 1861. In 1886 a cable tram line was opened from the ferry terminus at Milsons Point to Ridge Street in North Sydney. This was followed by the opening of Milsons Point Station in 1893, which was the terminus of the North Shore Line. The ferry terminal and station stood in the vicinity of the site of the north Harbour Bridge pylons, and were demolished to make way for the bridge. The ferry terminal disappeared into oblivion, but Milsons Point station re-opened in a new location on the west side of the Harbour Bridge approach with the opening of the bridge in 1932. A small passenger ferry still runs from Jeffrey Street Wharf on the east side of Bradfield park to Circular Quay.

Sydney Harbour Bridge

The pedestrian footway across the deck of the Harbour Bridge is accessible on the north side of the Harbour from the steps near the corner of Broughton Street and Ennis Road, Milsons Point. The view of Sydney Harbour from the Bridge is the most spectacular to be found anywhere short of going up in a helicopter.

A proposal by Francis Greenway in 1815 for a bridge to cross the Harbour from Dawes Point to the North Shore was the first of numerous proposals over the years for a harbour bridge. It wasn't until over a hundred years later on 28 July 1923 that the first sod was turned on the construction of a bridge designed by British engineers Ralph Freeman and Co to a specification drawn up by John Bradfield of the New South Wales Public Works Department.

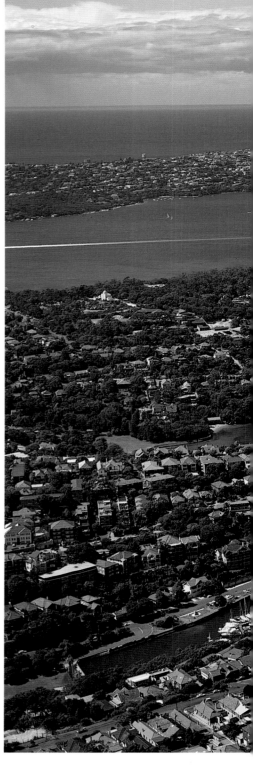

Completed in 1932, the Bridge, according to Laurence Ennis, Director of Construction for the contractors Dorman Long & Co of Middlesborough, was only possible at all at the time 'as a result of the advent of special steels'. Because Australia didn't possess the plant at the time to produce those steels,

most of the metal for the Bridge was forged in England, from ore mined in the Cleveland Hills 'where Captain Cook... was born and roamed as a boy.'

Sydney Harbour Bridge is the largest steel arch bridge in the world, but not the longest. New York's Bayonne Bridge at Staten Island, completed four months before the Harbour Bridge, is 1 metre longer at 510 metres, but is narrower, does not carry railway traffic and the weight of steel in its arch at 16,000 tons is less than a third that of the Sydney Bridge at 52,000 tons.

A steel staircase through the south east pylon of the Harbour Bridge

A ferry has just arrived at Old Cremorne Wharf on the right side of Mosman Bay in the above picture. Curraghbeena Point is at the head of the Bay on the left, while beyond it on the same side of the harbour are the Zoo and Bradleys Head.

leads up to a lookout and a display area with information about the Bridge and it's construction.

Beneath Bradfield Park at Milsons Point, runs Sydney's Harbour Tunnel, completed in 1992. The idea of a second harbour crossing was first suggested in the 1950's and various schemes were announced, then shelved, before construction of the tunnel was commenced in 1988.

Tunnels bored through sandstone, at the approaches at the north and south end of the tunnel are linked by pre-fabricated concrete sections, which were cast at Botany Bay, floated into position, then sunk into a trench excavated on the harbour bed and pieced together. The tunnel, costing $750 million and financed by a sudden dramatic increase in the bridge toll, was completed by a joint venture between Australian company Transfield and Japan's Kumagai Gumi.

Previous pages: The peninsular of Kirribilli with the Royal Botanic Gardens, Sydney City and the Harbour Bridge in the background.

Shell Cove (left) lies between Cremorne Point on the left and Kurraba Point on the right. Garden Island and the Eastern Suburbs are in the background.

The Royal Sydney Yacht Squadron at Kirribilli (right) is in the foreground of this view of Careening Cove. At the head of the Cove are the tall palm trees of Milson Park with the skyscrapers of North Sydney in the background.

Manly Jetcat passes Admiralty House on Kirribilli Point (right).

Neutral Bay (left). A submarine lies at the wharf of HMAS Platypus on the right side of the Bay. Kingsford Smith once landed and took off in his bi-plane from Anderson Park on the Bay at the bottom of the picture.

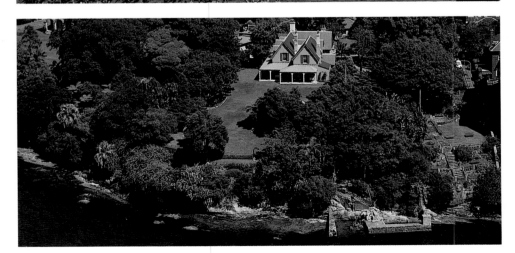

Kirribilli House (right) is the Prime Minister's official residence in Sydney.

Harbour peninsulars and forested valleys and headlands

Visit pockets of the original forest that coated the harbour foreshores on Balls Head and Berry Island and follow part of the Great North Walk along the valley of the Lane Cove River. Stroll the leafy streets and see the elegant stone houses of the peninsular suburb of Hunters Hill and visit the harbourside parks of the North Shore of the Parramatta River.

Lavender Bay

The aboriginal name for Lavender Bay, Quiberee, meaning 'fresh water' is carried on an 1850's house overlooking the bay on Lavender Street near Walker Street. Another aboriginal word, Warung, used as a general expression to describe the North Shore of the harbour and meaning 'the other side', is remembered in Warung Street near the bay. Henry Lawson Drive near Blues Point is named after the well known Australian writer and poet who used to live in the area. Lawson wrote of the horse ferry in 1913 that ran from Blues Point to Dawes Point and which he used to take into Sydney to work, 'The boats were high and flat and wouldn't steer. I have timed one to take three-quarters of an hour for the trip from Dawe's Point... when the steering gear or something went wrong, we'd have a trip round the harbour thrown in for our modest copper'.

In 1801 a Jamaican Negro, Billy Blue, arrived in Sydney after being sentenced to transportation for stealing a bag of sugar. Among his other achievements, Blue claimed to have fought with General Wolfe at Quebec in 1759 and to have been a spy for Cornwallis during the American War of Independence. He married in Sydney in 1805 and by 1807 was operating a ferry row-boat service from Millers Point to the point that now bears his name. Granted 80 acres in 1817 by Macquarie on the North Shore including Blues Point, which he called 'Northumberland Farm', Billy settled down in the area, fathered five children and lived on to a ripe old age. When he died on 8 May 1834, his obituary in the Sydney Morning Herald ran '(Died), on Monday last, at his residence Blue Point, Billy Blue, better known in Sydney as 'The Commodore', aged 95 years. Billy will long be remem-

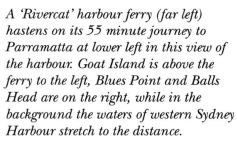

Previous pages: Lavender Bay is in the foreground on the right of this view of Sydney photographed from above North Sydney. A ferry is just about to arrive at McMahons Point Wharf on the right of the Bay. In front of the Opera House on the left of the picture the Manly Ferry starts its journey to Manly, while two ferries pass by in the opposite direction heading for Circular Quay.

A 'Rivercat' harbour ferry (far left) hastens on its 55 minute journey to Parramatta at lower left in this view of the harbour. Goat Island is above the ferry to the left, Blues Point and Balls Head are on the right, while in the background the waters of western Sydney Harbour stretch to the distance.

Two harbour ferries are about to pass either side of Goat Island in the picture above left. A convict built explosives magazine stands in the middle of the cluster of buildings on the right side of the Island. In the background are the cargo wharves of Millers Point and Darling Harbour and Sydney City skyline.

A closer view of the Island (left). Three hundred and fifty Maritime Services Board employees were once engaged in the boat yard and workshops on the Island, but these days the facilities are deserted and only a caretaker lives there.

bered by Australians for his eccentric though inoffensive disposition.' Billy had been granted his nickname of 'The Commodore' by Macquarie with instructions to keep his eye open for smugglers, but it was Billy Blue himself who was apprehended for smuggling Rum in 1818, and sentenced to a year 'polishing the King's iron with his eyebrows', (staring through the bars in gaol).

On 10 August 1824, the inward bound convict transport the *Phoenix* stuck fast on entering Sydney Harbour on the Sow and Pigs Reef between Camp Cove and Georges Head. The ship was refloated on the tide the following day, but was badly holed, condemned as unseaworthy, and became a prison hulk moored on the harbour to hold the so-called 'hard cases', transported convicts reconvicted of other crimes in Sydney. In the 1830's the *Phoenix* was moored in the bay between Blues Point and Milsons Point, and the bay became known for a time as 'Hulk Bay'. The ship's bosun, George Lavender, became a licensed ferryman on the harbour, and married Billy Blue's daughter Susannah in 1834. They lived in a stone cottage on land Susannah had inherited from her father. George became manager of the Old Commodore Inn, a hotel built in 1848 by Billy Blue's son John in memory of his father. George shot himself dead at the Inn in February 1851.

The Cavills

On the shore at the head of Lavender Bay used to be Cavill's Baths, founded by the English champion swimmer 'Professor' Fred Cavill, who emigrated to Australia with his family in 1879. He taught all his children to swim and their achievements in the sport, are the stuff of legends. To mention just a few of the exploits of some of his many children; Frederick junior won the New South Wales 1,000 yards championship at fifteen; Charles became the first man to swim across the Golden Gate in San Francisco in 1896, but drowned the following year in California giving an underwater swimming demonstration; Arthur, whose middle name was Channel as he was born the night his father was making his second unsuccessful attempt to swim the English Channel, also swam across San Francisco Harbour and is credited with inventing the "Australian crawl" swimming stroke. He died from the cold in 1914 attempting to swim across Seattle Harbour. His brother Dick was the first to use the crawl stroke in competitive swimming, won eighteen Australian Championships, and was the first man to swim 100 yards in under a minute. Another brother, Sydney Cavill, was also an Australian champion swimmer and invented the butterfly stroke. His daughter Madeleine, also an outstanding swimmer, was later awarded a medal for bravery by the Royal Humane Society along with her brothers Charles, Percy and Arthur Cavill.

Berrys Bay (top left). McMahons Point and Blues Point are on the left. In the background on the right are the old wharves on Walsh Bay.

The rugged rocky bushland of Balls Head Reserve (top left).

A weekend marquee in progress in the park at Berry Island Reserve (top right).

A Shell supertanker pumping out its cargo of crude oil into tanks on Gore Cove (above). Manns Point Park is on the left and the houses of the peninsular suburb of Greenwich stand behind the oil terminal.

Cavill's Baths no longer exist, but the swimming tradition of Lavender Bay lives on at North Sydney Olympic Pool, on the harbour next to the north west Harbour Bridge pylon. The baths, opened in 1936, were used for the 1938 British Empire Games, where five British Empire records and twenty four Australian records were set by Australian swimmers. Since the first world record was broken at the pool by the Australian Frank O'Neill in 1953, over 80 other world record times have been set there.

Luna Park

Luna Park fun park next to the baths, built on the site of the steel fabrication workshops for the Harbour Bridge, takes its name from the original Luna Park at Coney Island, New York. The first Australian Luna Park built at Glenelg South Australia, was dismantled, moved to it's present site, re-erected piece by piece and opened in 1935, complete with a sad clown's face at the entrance flanked by two towers lit by neon lights modelled on the Chrysler building New York. During the Second World War Luna Park's nightime illuminations were extinguished during the "brown out", then turned on again following the war using auxiliary power from the generators of a Dutch submarine the K2, moored alongside the park as an added walk through attraction. The neon lights on the entrance towers fused following their period of disuse in the war, and caught fire. A new happy (grotesque as some people called it) clowns face replaced the old one in 1950. Falling attendances at the park, not helped by a tragic fire in the ghost train in 1979, when one adult and seven children were burnt to death, led to the park being closed in the 1980's. However it has since been refurbished, complete with reproductions of the original Chrysler Building style entrance towers ready for a new generation of fun seekers.

These days Blues Point is dominated by a square block of apartments on the point built by local architect Harry Seidler. The Old Commodore Inn on Blues Point Road was demolished in 1973, to make way for the new red brick Old Commodore Tavern built on the same site. A stone cottage, so-called 'Billy Blues Cottage', built in the 1830's by Billy Blue for his son John, still exists at number 3 Commodore Crescent on Berrys Bay.

Goat Island

Thirteen acre Goat Island off Blues Point, known as 'Mel Mel' by the Aborigines, was quarried by convicts labouring in fetters in the early days of settlement for building stone for Sydney. Surveyor General Mitchell believed the Island was an excellent site for a fort to guard the approaches to the Upper Harbour and felt the work should cease in case the Island was 'quarried away'.

In 1833 convicts from the *Phoenix* were moved to huts on Goat Island where they laboured quarrying stone for naval stores, a wharf, guardhouse and magazine. Well-behaved felons were permitted to work without leg-irons, and Governor Bourke appointed a resident schoolmaster for the education of the convicts. The stone buildings constructed on the Island during the period 1833-38, with cedar doors and mahogany floors, are among the best preserved of the convict constructed buildings in Sydney. The magazine, 32 metres long and 10 metres wide, has walls nearly 2 metres thick and a beautifully crafted vaulted stone ceiling.

In 1838 the convicts were moved to Cockatoo Island and the buildings on Goat Island were manned by soldiers guarding the magazine and stores until 1893, when naval explosives were moved to Spectacle Island and army explosives to Newington armaments depot, the soldiers were withdrawn and the magazine was used to store civilian explosives, for

quarrying and mining companies.

When bubonic plague broke out in Sydney in 1900, the explosives were removed to hulks in Powder Hulk Bay and the Island taken over by the New South Wales Department of Health for use as an emergency bacteriological station. All staff in residence had to immediately leave, including the men of a water Police Station, which had been established on the Island since 1852. The arsenal was set up as a laboratory for the testing and diagnosis of samples infected by the plague and laboratory technicians and staff moved into the old soldiers quarters. As a result of their subsequent tests, Dr Ashburton Thompson and Dr Frank Tidswell were the first in the world to establish that bubonic plague was carried by fleas on rats and not by the rats themselves. (A claim subsequently disputed by the French who lodged a parallel claim at the same time).

These days the Island is under the control of the Maritime Services Board, who will happily supply information on tours.

Alexander Berry

Berrys Bay, west of Lavender Bay, is named after Alexander Berry, a Scottish merchant who started his shipping career working as a surgeon's mate for the East India Company. Leaving 'John Company' to pursue his own commercial interests, he became part owner of a ship the *City of Edinburgh*, and set sail for Sydney with a cargo that included 22,000 gallons of rum, arriving in Sydney on 13 January 1808, just thirteen days before Bligh was deposed in the Rum Rebellion on the 26th. Leaving Sydney at the end of 1809 with a cargo of hardwood for Cape Town, Berry was involved in many adventures on the way, including rescuing the survivors of a massacre by Maoris on a ship in Wangaroa Harbour New Zealand and having to put into Valparaiso in Chile for repairs after a rough voyage round-

ing Cape Horn. The *City of Edinburgh* then sank in the Atlantic, but Berry escaped in the ship's boat, reached the Azores and was on a vessel sailing from Lisbon to Cadiz in 1812 when he struck up an acquaintance with a fellow passenger Edward Wollstonecraft. Wollstonecraft, a cousin of Mary Wollstonecraft, the creator of Frankenstein, became Berry's agent, and they journeyed together to Sydney, arriving in 1819 to set up in business as merchants. Wollstonecraft received a land grant of 200 hectares on the north shore, where in 1820 he built a small cottage called 'Crows Nest', after which the present day suburb near North Sydney is named. In 1827 Berry mar-

ried his partner's sister Elizabeth Wollstonecraft. Her brother Edward died in 1832, and Elizabeth planned a new 'Crows Nest House' opposite McLaren Street on the present day Pacific Highway. Elizabeth died during it's construction and Alexander lived there on his own until 1873, when he died at the age of ninety two. The house was demolished in 1929, however the walls and gates, decorated with the design of a ship's crows nest and birds nest in the wrought ironwork, remain.

Berry's trading ships used to anchor in 'Berry's Bay' and the neighbouring suburb of Wollstonecraft is named after his business partner and brother-in-law.

Balls Head Bay on the left and Gore Cove on the right are separated by Berry Island Reserve. On the opposite side of the harbour are Snails Bay and Mort Bay on the north shore of Balmain.

Onions Point, Woolwich separates the waters of the Lane Cove River on the right from those of the Parramatta River on the left. The Point is named after the Sydney merchant Samuel Onions who bought land on the point in 1835. Convicted of perjury in July 1836 after suing a man called Raine for assault then falsely swearing that Raine owed him money, Onions was sentenced to seven years hard labour at Norfolk Island Penal Settlement.

Balls Head

Balls Head, named after Lieutenant Henry Ball, commander of *HMS Supply* of the First Fleet, is an elevated bushland reserve with spectacular views towards Balmain, Goat Island, the city and Harbour Bridge. The headland, made a public reserve in 1926, has a circular drive around the crown and several trails leading through tree studded and rocky bushland terrain to grassy clearings with picnic tables and barbecues. The waters off Balls Head, are some of the deepest in the Harbour, with a depth of 38 metres.

Naval patrol boats from *HMAS Waterhen* on nearby Balls Head Bay,

were used in the ABC television series 'Patrolboat'. The massive raised platform of a coal storage facility next to the naval base, now in disuse, was created as a supply facility for coal burning steamers and was last used to store coal ready for shipment to Sydney's harbourside industries and power stations.

Berry Island on the west side of Balls Head Bay was originally an island on part of Alexander Berry's estate which he linked to the mainland by a stone causeway. The island became a park in 1926, and was joined to the mainland by a proper landbridge in the form of an extensive grassy park in the 1960's. The

former island is an interesting pocket of natural bushland on the Harbour, with a path around the perimeter leading through tall stands of gnarled angophora trees past aboriginal middens and rock engravings.

Gore Cove

Neighbouring Gore Cove is named after William Gore, Provost Marshall to Governor Bligh. On the arrest of Bligh during the "Rum Rebellion" of 1808, Gore, as one of Bligh's supporters, was taken prisoner by the conspirators and transported to Newcastle, where he worked as forced labour alongside other convicts in the coal mines. Re-instated in office by Macquarie, who granted him 150 acres in the nearby suburb of 'Gore Hill' in 1810, then dismissed again, Gore also served time in debtors' prison and was later up on charges of shooting and wounding a man.

The oil terminal on Gore Cove, was originally the first oil refinery to be built in Australia, designed by a Scottish oil engineer John Fell in 1903 for the British Imperial Oil Company. These days it is an oil storage facility belonging to Shell, where supertankers pump their cargoes into storage tanks onshore ready to be pumped by a pipeline on the har-

Gore Creek Bay at Northwood on the Lane Cove River. In the background is the convoluted shoreline of the waterway that Governor Phillip called the harbour of 'a hundred bays.'

bour bed to the oil refinery further up the harbour at Auburn.

Greenwich

Neighbouring Greenwich is not named after the suburb on the River Thames where Governor Phillip attended college, but after a house. A boat builder, George Green, received one of the original land grants at Greenwich in 1836. He lived in a house built that year at the corner of George Street and St Lawrence Street which still stands today. A later owner of the house, Captain Kerr Mann, named the house Greenwich. The park at Manns Point, with the remains of old stone wharves at the waters edge, is on the site of a salt and copra bond store known as the Salt Bond, which burned down in 1917. Ferry services operate from the wharf at Greenwich Point to Circular Quay.

The first tunnel excavated beneath the Harbour extends from Long Nose Point Balmain to Manns

Point Greenwich. Constructed between 1913 and 1924 to carry electricity cables beneath the Harbour for the North Shore tram system, the tunnel was necessary because previous cables layed on the harbour bed, had been snagged by ships dragging their anchors.

A considerable feat of engineering and a hazardous operation at the time; the Harbour waters twice broke in during excavation through fissures in the rock, the tunnel, 1,760 feet long, was described by a reporter from the Sun newspaper just before it's opening in 1924. 'The atmosphere was cool and pleasant, electric light bulbs twinkled like golden glow worms, and here and there the water trickled slowly in from the roof and sides... On the level of the tunnel it is possible to walk upright with ease. In fact two or three men could walk abreast.'

The cables in the tunnel remained in use to supply electricity to the North Shore until 1969 when other supplies became available from power stations on the Central Coast.

A picturesque track follows an old timber-getters trail from River Road Greenwich past "Lilly Pilly Falls" and through Gore Creek Reserve to a sports ground on the harbour at a bay called Gore Creek.

Longueville west of Greenwich,

The Lane Cove River (above) with Linley Point and Hunters Hill on the left and Burns Bay and the suburb of Riverview in the centre of the picture.

St Ignatius College dominates the headland of Riverview at the centre left of the picture (left). Beyond Riverview are Tambourine Bay and the winding shore of the suburb of Longueville. Meandering along the opposite side of the Lane Cove River on the right is the shore-line of Hunters Hill.

was once part of a 150 acre land grant belonging to Rupert Kirk he called 'Woodford Park'. Kirk established a factory on his land in 1831 for refining oil and sugar and making vinegar, soap and candles. The factory was still in operation in the 1840's. Woodford Bay between Longueville and Northwood is named after his property.

Tambourine Bay

There's a good little bushwalk that starts near Longueville on River Road West, descends through the bush of Warrarroon Reserve passing unusual rock formations and an old shale mine, to come out at the mangroves on Tambourine Bay. The bay is named after Tambourine Nell, a woman in great demand as a tambourine player at the "Sailors Home" she maintained at Dawes Point, who fell foul of the law, took refuge in a cave on the bay, and lived for a time there as a fugitive before she was arrested and brought to justice. The walking track continues around Tambourine Bay past Tambourine Bay Reserve, a grassy park with swings and a barbecue area, to follow the foreshore through the bush below Riverview College to Burns Bay. To return to civilisation, walk through the grounds of the college to Riverview Street.

Riverview

The area around Riverview and the Lane Cove River was the haunt of deserting soldiers, sailors and criminals in the old days, described as the 'resort of disreputable people... as great a set of ruffians as the Colony holds'. The Sydney Gazette in the 1840's called the region 'an abode of murderers', and a permanent garrison of troops was stationed on Woodford Bay for the protection of the settlers. Burns Bay was known as 'Murdering Bay' at this time.

The original land owner at Riverview was Manuel Johnson, who built a house called Riverview Cottage, where he lived with his wife

from 1866 to 1876. Between them they created a beautiful garden with trees, shrubs and a rockery, which still exists in the grounds of Riverview College. The college, (it's official name is St Ignatius), was founded by an Irish Catholic priest, Father Joseph Dalton in 1880 at a time when Dalton described the area as still 'terra-incognita', with just wild bush cut through with deep gullies and winding inlets.

The Lane Cove River

'Lane Cove' was mentioned in William Bradley's journal on February 2 1788, six days after the First Fleet landed at Sydney Cove,

Tarban Creek and Tarban Creek Bridge are in the foreground of the picture above, flanked by Hunters Hill on the left and Wrights Point on the right. Five Dock Bay and the suburb of Drummoyne lie beyond the arch of Gladesville Bridge in the middle distance on the right.

The Lane Cove River (right) in the Lane Cove River State Recreation Area.

The meandering tree-lined course of the Lane Cove River between Epping Road Bridge and Fullers Bridge in Willoughby (far right).

The Lane Cove River (below) with the thick bushland of Boronia Park on the right and the suburb of Linley Point on the left. On the far side of the Figtree Bridge on the left is the pointed tower of Mary Reibey's House.

The graceful arch of the Gladesville Bridge (right) was the longest concrete arch span in the world when it was completed in 1964.

The Victoria Road - Burns Bay Road interchange at Huntleys Point at the north end of the Gladesville Bridge (below right). In the background are Tarban Creek and Tarban Creek Bridge.

making it one of the earliest place-names bestowed on the Harbour. At that time what was assumed to be a cove was sighted from the harbour, but further explorations revealed the cove was in fact the mouth of the Lane Cove River. It is generally assumed the placename was given because the Lane Cove River winds between the bush on the banks of the Harbour like an English lane through the hedgerows, but it could also have been named after John Lane, the son of the Lord Mayor of London and a good friend of Arthur Phillip.

The Lane Cove River area is the second most extensive stretch of natural bushland still remaining on the Harbour after Davidson Park north of the Roseville Bridge. There is a wide variety of scenery along the river banks, from spectacular over-hanging rock shelters and sheltered rocky gullies with ferns and moss covering the rocks, to deep rock pools where you can cool off on a hot day and open forested areas crossed by old logging trails. From Boronia Avenue at Hunters Hill it's possible to walk along the entire length of the Lane Cove River Valley, crossing some main roads on the way, to Lorna Pass in Pennant Hills, some twelve hours and 25 kilometres away. If you had the inclination you could even continue for a further 230 kilometres to Newcastle, for the walk is a section of the 'Great North Walk' which has it's official starting place at Valentia Street Wharf Hunters Hill and pushes through the bush all the way to Newcastle on the Hunter River.

From Boronia Avenue the track skirts the shore of the harbour, past groves of paperbark trees and on boardwalks over the mangroves to the attractive grassy park of Buffalo Creek Reserve. The creek passing through the reserve was named by Captains Raven and Kent, two of the original land holders of the district, after *HMS Buffalo*, the ship they sailed out in.

Further upstream on Buffalo Creek, on the other side of Pittwater

Road, is the Field of Mars Wildlife Refuge, created originally by Governor King as the Field of Mars Common for owners of nearby land grants to graze livestock. The refuge has parking spaces, picnic areas with barbecues, a visitor centre and a bushwalk through tall stands of ancient eucalypts. A great tract of the north shore between Rydalmere and Artarmon was once known as 'The Field of Mars' after Phillip gave that title to land grants he made to military officers in the region. Phillip seems to have coined the phrase as a jesting reference to The Field of Mars in ancient Greece. Mars was the god of war, but that could have been little consolation to the men of the military who initially found their new won land offered about as much prospect of cultivation as a field on Mars.

On the Lane Cove River the track continues north for several kilometres through dense bushland, passing an occasional aboriginal midden; large heaps of shells embedded in a black ash soil that are the remains of aboriginal camp fires, through Magdala Park, to cross a pedestrian bridge over the River near the end of Magdala Road. At nearby Epping Road Bridge, it is necessary to re-cross on the bridge to the west side of the River to continue on the bush track. This section of the walk passes through 'Fairyland', a clearing in the bush which was an organised picnic grounds in days gone by . Hundreds of revellers would descend every weekend by launch from Fig Tree Bridge or by private boat to 'Fairyland Tea Gardens' where there was a park with a cricket pitch, a children's playground and wooden picnic shelters. The odd piece of rubble and corrugated iron scattered among palms and camphor laurels that were once part of the gardens is all that survives of the old 'Fairyland'.

Lane Cove River Park

Between Fullers Bridge and De Burghs Bridge is the 400 hectare

Lane Cove River Park, with extensive picnic and barbecue areas, canoes and boats available for hire and an old fashioned paddle-wheeler, the Turrumburra, plying up and down the river carrying passengers on pleasure trips. The Lane Cove River is quite broad on the section through the park as it's waters are held back by a weir just upstream from Fullers Bridge. The region was dedicated as a public park in 1938 and the roads paths and facilities created through relief work during the depression.

On the north side of the Lane Cove River, near the entrance to the park off Lady Game Drive, is a Visitor Centre and a small enclosure called the Kukundi Wildlife Shelter. In the shelter are several species of Australian wildlife, including echidnas, wallabies, wombats and a variety of birdlife. Also nearby is the kitchen of the Jenkins homestead, circa 1860, all that remains after the house burnt down in 1924. Thomas Jenkins and his wife Maria, who lived there with his thirteen children, was one of five orchardists who had property along this stretch of the Lane Cove River in the mid-nineteenth century. Thomas transported his fruit to Sydney on the Nellie, a steamer he had built himself which he used on weekends to bring day trippers up the Lane Cove River, where members of his family took sightseers on walks to the many beauty spots lining the river banks.

Further upstream on the same side of the river, Fiddens Wharf Reserve is close to the site of a wharf established by an ex-convict Joseph Fidden. Fidden, a gunsmith by trade,

Looking Glass Point at the centre of the picture with beyond it on the same side of the Parramatta River, Looking Glass Bay, Bedlam Point and the suburb of Henley, named after a village on the Thames in Oxfordshire.

was transported for seven years for stealing a tin pot, two loaves of bread and a pot of paint. Granted 16 hectares by Macquarie in the area in 1821, Fidden established himself as a riverman, rowing logs to Sydney brought to his wharf by the timber-getters upriver and delivering provisions to the isolated river settlements on the return trip. Fidden later moved to Sydney, and died in Kent Street in April 1856 at the age of 99. A pub called the Sawyers Arms stood at the end of Fiddens Wharf Road in the 1840's. A saw mill was still in operation on the Lane Cove River near DeBurghs bridge until the 1960's. The wood burning steam powered electricity generator that provided power for the mill is now a working exhibit in the Powerhouse Museum at Darling Harbour.

On the north side of DeBurghs Bridge the walk continues on the east side of the river. After a few kilometres the track reaches Browns Waterhole close to the end of Kissing Point Road in South Turramurra, an important log trail junction in the pioneering days. Another interesting landmark further north up the valley on the west side is 'Whale Rock', a sandstone formation bearing an uncanny resemblance to a whale which even has an eye. The rock is on a track that follows Devlins Creek to Sutherland Road Epping.

The main track, however, continues on the east side of the river for five or six kilometres, eventually reaching Lorna Pass, a section of track built to provide relief work during the depression and named after Miss Lorna Brand who was instrumental in raising money to finance the project. At the end of Lorna Pass the track returns to civilisation at the busy Comennara Parkway in Pennant Hills.

Hunters Hill

Hunters Hill, a peninsula 5 kilometres long and an average of 2 kilometres wide, divides the waters of the Lane Cove and Parramatta Rivers.

The aborigines called the area Mookaboola, 'the meeting of the waters', a name preserved in the Municipality's coat of arms. The last living member of the Kameraigal tribe living in the area, 'Black Lucy', had a two-roomed house provided by the town, but she used it for her animals and continued living in her native gunyah until she died in 1920. Hunters Hill was once a general expression used to describe a large tract of land on the north shore of the harbour after Captain Hunter of the First Fleet ship the *Sirius*. With the creation of the district of Ryde west of the Lane Cove River and of Willoughby, east of it, only the residue of the district at todays Hunters Hill remained to carry on the name.

An early land owner in the area was Mary Reiby, who purchased some of the first Crown Land at Hunters Hill in December 1839. Under her maiden name of Mary Haydock at the age of thirteen, living as an orphan with her grandmother in England, Reiby had been sentenced to seven years transportation for going on a joy-ride on a carthorse without first asking the owner's permission. In Sydney when she was seventeen she married a ship's officer, Thomas Reiby, who went on to become a successful shipowner and merchant. When Thomas Reiby died in 1811 leaving Mary to bring up their seven children, she took on and expanded her late husband's business interests and became one of the richest people in the colony. The land she bought at Hunters Hill, opposite Linley Point, had a large native fig tree growing in the grounds, and she named the weekend cottage she built there 'Figtree House'.

Another landowner at Hunters Hill in the 1830's was John Tawell, a zealous Quaker who in 1836 bought 492 gallons of rum and 116 gallons of gin which he ceremoniously poured into the harbour at Sydney Cove. After returning to England he

was tried for murder in 1845 and hanged.

In 1841 a seventeen year old Frenchman, Jules Joubert, arrived in Sydney as a cadet on board a French corvette and found a job at the French Consulate. As Jules later wrote, 'I had made up my mind to settle down, in order to do so, I looked about for some land having a prospective value'. Working with his brother Didier who had arrived in Sydney in 1839, and seventy stonemasons and tradesmen, many of them artisans brought out under contract from Lombardy in Italy, the Jouberts bought up land in Hunters Hill including Mary Reiby's property,

and set about building houses from the local sandstone. Many of the houses they built, standing in their own grounds, surrounded by stone walls, still exist today. Jules Joubert pressed his steam yacht, the *Ysobel*, into service as a ferry to bring residents to and from Sydney and later became the first Mayor of the Municipality of Hunters Hill while his brother Didier was the first Chairman of Council.

Many of the houses at Hunters Hill have a story behind them. Some carry aboriginal names, such as Warrawillah, 'swirling waters', Kaota, 'eventide', and Gunagulla, 'sky or heaven'. A wooden house in Yerton

Avenue is the only survivor of four Austrian pre-fabricated houses brought out by a French settler Etienna Bordier from the Paris exhibition of 1854. 'Passy' a house built by Jules Joubert in 1858 for the French Consul General Louis Sentis, is the origin of the house used by Barnard Eldershaw in the book 'A House is Built'.

Clarkes Point Reserve and neighbouring Morts Reserve at the south east corner of Woolwich on the Hunters Hill peninsula, have picnic and barbecue areas with beautiful views looking across to Birchgrove and the city. The area was once an industrial site belonging to the

Mort's Dock and Engineering Company. A nearby dry dock excavated from solid sandstone between 1898 to 1902, 850 feet long, 80 feet wide and with a draught of 26 feet was the biggest graving dock built in Australia at the time and could take the biggest ships in the world of that era. It is now used by the Army's Water Transport Squadron. The remains of slipways can be seen in the park at Mort's Reserve where many ships were built over the years, including some of the Manly Ferry steamers. Onions Point at the very tip of Woolwich is named after the Sydney merchant Samuel Onions who bought land there in 1835.

Onions was convicted of perjury the following year and sentenced to seven years transportation to Norfolk Island.

When the Burns Bay Road interchange, cutting across the western section of Hunters Hill peninsula was built in the 1960's, some of the region's old buildings went with it. Jules Joubert's own cottage, 'St Malo', named after his mother's birthplace in Brittany, was among those demolished. However other buildings were saved. Mary Reibey's house, which had been added to and improved upon by the Jouberts, was moved slightly east, and still occupies a position overlooking the Lane

Cove River at Reiby Street Hunters Hill close to the southern end of the Figtree Bridge. The Anglican All Saints Church dating to the 1850's built in nearby Church Street and known as the 'Fig Tree Chapel', was moved stone by stone to a new site on Figtree Road.

Gladesville

A convict, John Glade, used to own land at present day Gladesville and the bay on his property was soon known as Glade's Bay. However the suburb only became known as Gladesville when the area was subdivided for housing in the 1880's. Off the shore at Henley, south

Gladesville, stands a monument in the shape of a broken off column on the Three Brothers Rocks. Since 1858 sculling races have taken place on a 3 mile 176 yard course from Shepherds Point near the present day Ryde Bridge to 'The Brothers' rocks. In 1888, 22 year old Henry Searle from the Clarence River, took on all-comers on the course, and even though he'd never raced in scullers before, beat all the current Australian champions and smashed the course record. He then accepted a challenge to race against an American for the world championship on the Thames in London. He also won that race, and was on his way home to Australia when he contracted enteric fever on board ship. Rushed to hospital when his ship berthed in Melbourne, he died there of peritonitis in December 1889. When Searle's coffin passed through the streets of Sydney from the railway station to the Clarence River Steamer on the harbour, it is estimated that a quarter of a million people thronged the streets to pay their last respects. Public donations raised the funds to build a monument to Searle at the finishing line of the course where he first achieved his fame, which now became known as the "Ryde Bridge to Searle's Monument" course.

Bedlam Point on Punt Road next to Banjo Patterson Park was called 'Bethlem Point' by John Glade and its name became contracted by popular usage. In 1820 a lunatic asylum whose inmates comprised mostly the criminally insane under the watchful eye of a platoon of soldiers was established at the point. The Bedlam Point asylum was closed in 1829, and a new much larger mental hospital later established at Gladesville on a raised site overlooking the Parramatta River a little further east.

Looking Glass Point directly west of Bedlam Point was named on 15th February 1788, when Governor Phillip stopped there during an exploration of the harbour. As Lieutenant Bradley wrote in his journal; 'We stopped at a neck of land for breakfast. We were soon met there by a native armed... (who) examined everything very attentively and went into all our boats from one to the other... The Governor gave this man a hatchet, and a looking-glass, which, when he looked into, he looked immediately behind the glass, to see if any person was there, and then pointed to the glass and the shadows which he saw in the water, signifying they were similar.'

The suburb of Tennyson, west of Glades Bay, is named after Hallam Lord Tennyson, Governor of South Australia 1899 to 1902 and Governor General of the Commonwealth of Australia from 1902 to 1904. He was the son of the poet Alfred Lord Tennyson who penned the Charge of the Light Brigade. 'Ours is not to reason why, ours is but to do or die.'

Kissing Point

Kissing Point, on the harbour in the suburb of Putney, was named because ships heading upstream would frequently touch or 'kiss' the harbour bottom near the point, and have to unload their goods or transfer them to shallow draught lighters to continue the journey to Parramatta. For fifty years from the 1790's commercial citrus orchards in the Kissing Point area supplied fruit to Sydney. The orchards were established originally from the seeds of fruit bought by the Reverend Richard Johnson in Rio de Janeiro on his voyage out with the First Fleet.

Early settlers in the area were the convict John Small and his wife Mary, who for their faithful service to the Governor as house servants were granted land at Kissing Point in 1793. Small was a successful farmer and later inn-keeper at Kissing Point. Their daughter Rebecca, born in Sydney in September 1788, laid claim to being the first white child born in Australia. In 1807 she married Francis Oakes, the head constable at Parramatta and after bearing him twelve children, lived on at Parramatta to the age of ninety five. James Squire, another early resident, was a free settler from Kent who was granted land at Kissing Point in 1795. On the farm he established he grew barley, built a malthouse, and became Australia's first brewer, producing his first alcoholic beverage in 1800 and cutting Australia's first hops in 1806. He opened a hotel on his property, 'The Malting Shovel' and built a big house next to his brewery. Bennelong the Aborigine spent his last days in a humpy in the grounds of the house, died and was buried there in 1815. Bennelong Park on the waterfront north of the Point is named after him. Squire's son, James Squire Farnell, went on to become Premier of New South Wales.

Ryde

In the 1840's a free settler G.M.Pope opened a general store at Kissing Point Village which he called the 'Ryde Store' after his birthplace in the Isle of Wight. Pope and some of the other residents of Kissing Point disliked having mail addressed from England to a place with such a peculiar placename and campaigned successfully to have the name of the Post Office changed to 'Ryde Post Office' in 1846. It wasn't long before the name of Kissing Point fell into disuse and became all but obliterated when Kissing Point village and the surrounding area was incorporated into the Municipality of Ryde in 1870. However the old place name lives on in eight Kissing Point Roads, in the area bordered by Parramatta, Turramurra and Ermington.

The Ryde Railway Bridge spanning the Parramatta River at Ryde, with a height of 38 feet above the water at high tide, makes an effective barrier for tall ships wishing to proceed any further upstream. The bridge, connecting Sydney by rail with Epping, Hornsby and Newcastle, was opened in 1886. Work started in 1947 on work on a new rail-

way bridge directly east of the old one, but construction was abandoned during the economic slump of 1954. Work on the new bridge resumed in 1975 with a different design to that proposed in 1947, but using the abutments and piers already completed when work ceased in 1954. The new bridge opened in 1980. A cycling and jogging track follows the harbour shore through Meadowbank Park from the north west end of the bridge. The original Ryde road bridge was completed in 1935 to replace a vehicle punt ferry.

Rydalmere

For the last six kilometres of its course beyond Ermington, the Parramatta river is a narrow channel 200 metres wide between mudbanks. Along much of this section of the Harbour the land on the water is occupied by industry or housing, there are however some parks, including a continuous 6 kilometre stretch of reserve with walking and cycle tracks on the north shore of the Harbour between Ermington and a pedestrian footbridge over the Harbour at Park Road Rydalmere.

Rydalmere received it's name in 1886 from a real estate agent who bought up farming land in the area and sub-divided and re-sold it for housing, naming it after a lake in Cumbria in England's Lake District.

In April 1791 Governor Phillip granted 40 acres of land in the area to Philip Schaeffer, a German free settler who had arrived with the Second Fleet in July 1790 and had fought on the British side during the American War of Independence. Schaeffer cleared the ground on his grant, planted grapevines, and within a few years was producing Australia's first wine from his property which he called 'The Vineyard'.

The site of Schaeffer's farm is marked by Vineyard Creek, which runs south through Rydalmere to the Parramatta River near the railway bridge next to Rydalmere Hospital. On the riverbank close to the south

Mangroves still line the shore of the Parramatta River at Ermington (above). Just beyond the line of mangroves on the left is the wharf of the Royal Australian Navy's Newington Armaments Depot.

side of the bridge is a neatly maintained grave with the inscription, 'In this grave lie the remains of Elinor Magee and her infant child, who were drowned in the Parramatta River January 1773.

81

PARRAMATTA TO DARLING HARBOUR

Historical buildings and Darling Harbour

Visit the colonial relics of Australia's second oldest settlement and see the sports facilities for the year 2000 Olympics. Explore Homebush Bicentennial Park and the grounds of one of Sydney's last harbourside mansions. Spend a day in the gardens, museums and shops of Darling Harbour.

Rose Hill

Parramatta, 27 kilometres as the crow flies or 32 kilometres by the harbour channel from the heads, is the second oldest settlement in Australia.

In April 1788 Governor Phillip set out from Sydney Cove with a boat expedition intent on travelling to the navigable limit of Sydney Harbour, then 'penetrating into the country westward, as far as seven days provision would permit' to search for an area suitable as a farming settlement. The expedition reached the head of the harbour on 24 April, described by Surgeon John White as the place where 'the tide ceased to flow and all further progress for boats was stopped by a flat space of large broad stones over which a freshwater stream ran.' Phillip penetrated as far inland as present day Prospect near Blacktown before re-tracing his tracks, choosing a site for a new settlement on some rising ground close to the tidal limit of the harbour at a place he named Rose Hill after George Rose, Secretary of the Admiralty.

Six months later, on 2 November 1788, Phillip, accompanied by his surveyor Baron Alt, eleven marines and ten convicts, camped at 'Rose Hill' and set to work clearing the ground and marking out the streets for a new settlement. Two years later a farm had been established planted with 200 acres of cereal crops. Forty one huts

Previous pages: Darling Harbour and the City.

The head of Sydney Harbour at Parramatta (far left). The stone Lennox Bridge at the bottom of the picture, completed by the Scottish stonemason David Lennox in 1839, was the first bridge over Sydney Harbour and is one of the oldest bridges in Australia. In the middle distance on the right is Rosehill Racecourse.

Industrial establishments line each side of the Parramatta River (left) at Rydalmere on the left and Camellia on the right. In the foreground is the road bridge for James Ruse Drive and Camellia Railway Bridge.

Silverwater Bridge in the foreground (left) with the Shell Oil Refinery and Duck River in the background. The upper course of the Duck River passes through the suburb of Auburn, named after the poem, 'Sweet Auburn loveliest village of the plain' by Oliver Goldsmith.

The portico of the Kings School Parramatta (above), on the north shore of the Parramatta River on O'Connell Street. The first buildings at the school were completed in 1836. The school has now moved to North Parramatta and the old school buildings are currently owned by the New South Wales Department of Health.

The stately Soldiers Memorial (below left) in Parramatta Park, built from four sandstone Doric columns from the 1837 Parramatta Courthouse, was erected in memory of men from the Parramatta district who were killed in the Boer War.

Lancer Barracks (above) on Station Street, built by Macquarie in 1820, is the oldest existing military building in Australia and the home of the New South Wales Lancers. Linden House in the grounds, dating to 1828, houses the Regimental Museum.

The Tudor style gatehouse (below) at the entrance to Parramatta Park at the end of George Street, was erected in 1885. In the park just inside the gates on the right is the 'Fitzroy Tree' against which Lady Fitzroy the wife of the Governor was thrown from her carriage and killed in 1847.

Old Government House Parramatta (above), the oldest public building in Australia, was originally erected on the site in 1790. A new house incorporating parts of the old building was completed in 1799, and further additions were made by Macquarie in 1815. The National Trust restored the building and it was officially opened to the public by the Queen in 1970.

St Johns Anglican Church (below) on Church Street Parramatta dates to 1855. The original church on the site was opened in 1803. A gravestone in the original graveyard on O'Connell Street, that of Henry Dodd, who died in 1791, is the oldest gravestone in Australia.

had been built, each housing ten or twelve convicts, as well as, according to Captain Watkin Tench, 'several small huts where convict families of good character are allowed to reside.' The Governor had a 'lath and plaister' house, and more substantial buildings were under construction using bricks from a kiln which employed 52 convicts and produced 25,000 bricks a week.

Parramatta

The Aborigines called the head of the Harbour where the stream cascaded over 'large broad stones', "Parramatta", meaning 'the place where the eels jump' or 'the place where the eels lie down'. In honour of the Aboriginal name for the area, Phillip changed the name of his settlement from Rose Hill to Parramatta in June 1791, while the farming district continued to be known as Rose Hill. Parramatta became for a time a bigger town than Sydney, with a population of 1,970 in 1792 compared with only 1,170 in Sydney at that time. As one of the early chroniclers summed up the situation, 'Sydney has long been considered as only a depot for stores... and all our strength transferred to Rose Hill.'

During the expedition of April 1788, White had noted in his journal on the 25th that near the head of the Harbour, 'The trees around us were immensely large and the tops of them filled with loraquets and paroquets of exquisite beauty, which chattered to such a degree that we could scarcely hear each other speak.' The first settlers later called the birds 'Rose Hillers' which said quickly, sounded like "Rosellas", the word that has been used ever since for the small brightly coloured lorikeets with yellow beaks first described by Surgeon White and still found in numerous numbers in many parts of New South Wales.

These days there is plenty to see from the old colonial days in Parramatta, which, while it is not the biggest settlement in Sydney any more, is at the demographic heart of the greater Sydney region. The local football team incidentally, is nicknamed "The Eels".

The city of Parramatta is connected to Sydney by train, (Australia's first train track) and by ferry (the first harbour ferry ran from Sydney to Parramatta).Though there has never been any interruption to the train service - except for strikes - since the line opened in 1855, the Parramatta ferry ceased operation for 65 years from 1928 until the service re-opened with fast 'river-cats' in December 1993.

Left. The facilities for the year 2000 Olympics at Homebush, with the Olympic Stadium on the left, the Olympic Pool in the centre and the warm-up track on the right. In the background is Homebush Bicentennial Park and the waters of Sydney Harbour.

The first ferry on the run was the *Rose Hill Packet*, launched in 1789 in a ship yard on the west side of Sydney Cove and used according to Lieutenant Bradley 'for carrying stores and provisions over the flats to Rose Hill'. The *Rose Hill Packet* could take days in unfavourable conditions to make the return journey to Parramatta, in spite of convicts labouring like galley slaves to help propel the boat and she was nicknamed "the lump" for being so slow and unseaworthy.

Governor Macquarie's Lancer Barracks at 2 Smith Street, completed in 1820, is still in use today by the army and has the Linden House regimental museum in the grounds. Nearby St John's Cemetery is the oldest existing in Australia and contains the country's oldest headstone, that of Henry Dodd, who died in 1791.

In Parramatta Park, Old Government House is open to the public. The first House for Governor Phillip was built in 1790, a second House incorporating part of the existing building was completedold in 1799 and had additions made by Macquarie in 1815. It is the oldest public building in Australia. Old Government House was used by the Kings School as a junior house from 1910 to the 1960's. The Kings School, on the opposite bank of the Parramatta River on O'Connell Street, was opened by the Anglican church in 1832. Some of the school buildings, now owned by the Government, date to 1836. Also started in 1836 was the stone Lennox Bridge at Church Street on the harbour side of the weir at the head of the Harbour. Designed and built by John Lennox, a Scottish stonemason

The waterways and mangroves of Homebush Bicentennial Park (top).

One of several ship's hulks (above) that lie on the harbour bed in the shallow waters of Homebush Bay.

who emigrated to New South Wales in 1832, it was the first bridge over Sydney Harbour.

Also in Parramatta Park are the remains of Governor Brisbane's Observatory, and a striking monument to Australians killed in the Boer War. The 'Fitzroy Tree', in Parramatta Park near the Tudor Gatehouse at the end of George Street, is the tree against which Lady Mary Fitzroy, wife of Governor Fitzroy, was thrown and killed when her carriage overturned in Parramatta Park in 1847.

In March 1791 Phillip made the first land grant of 30 acres to an ex-convict, James Ruse, to establish how long a land holder took to become self-sufficient starting with an area of uncleared ground. Experiment Farm Cottage on the site, built by Surgeon John Harris in the 1830's, is open to the public on Ruse Street. James Ruse later married Elizabeth Perry, the first woman convict to receive her freedom in Australia.

Lieutenant John Macarthur arrived in Sydney with his wife Elizabeth in June 1790 with the Second Fleet. Macarthur was a pioneer in establishing and creating an export trade for the merino wool industry in Australia. He received a land grant of 100 acres at Parramatta in 1793. The stone house he built on his property, named 'Elizabeth Farm' after his wife, is open to the public on Alice Street. It is the oldest house in Australia. Many of the original interior Georgian joinery fittings remain intact inside the house.

The woollen textile industry in Australia was first established in 1801 at the women's convict barracks in Parramatta, where the prisoners were employed spinning and weaving woollen cloth. The barracks, called the 'Female Factory', were nicknamed by the inmates "the Black Hole of Parramatta". The mill employed 1200 convicts and continued in operation in that role until the 1840's. A high quality tweed the convicts produced was copied by Bradford woollen mills in England and is still marketed today as 'Parramatta Cloth'. The buildings of the Female Factory on the north bank of the Parramatta River, are now in the grounds of a hospital.

The Duck River

Close to the Silverwater Bridge, the harbour channel splits into two, the Parramatta River leading to Parramatta, and the Duck River leading to the suburbs of Granville and Auburn. Captain Hunter was probably close to the junction during the first exploration of the Harbour when he recorded on the 5th February 1788, 'At noon, we were far enough to see the termination of the Harbour as far as navigable for ships, being all flats above us, with narrow passages that we supposed might run a considerable distance, but very shoal.'

At the junction of the Parramatta and Duck rivers is the Shell Oil Refinery, established in the 1920's on part of John Macarthur's former estate. The refinery was supplied with crude oil from a fleet of flat bottomed barges which commuted from the oil storage tanks at Gore Bay 15 kilometres downstream, until Gore Bay was connected to the refinery by a pipeline on the harbour bed.

During Phillip's expedition to the head of the Harbour in April 1788, Surgeon John White wrote in his journal on the 17th of April 'When we got as far back as the arm or branch of the sea which forms the upper part of Port Jackson Harbour, we saw many ducks, but could not get within shot of any of them.' The 'Duck River' was subsequently marked on Captain Hunter's first chart of the Harbour in 1788. The 'ducks' were probably swamp hens, and water hens, then common in the area and which feature today on the Auburn Council's coat of arms.

In the upper reaches of the Duck River a two and a half kilometre walking track follows the riverbank from Factory Street Auburn to Wellington Road, passing through various parks on the way including the Auburn Botanic Gardens, and neighbouring Japanese Gardens.

The industrial suburb of Rhodes on the east shore of Homebush Bay is named after a mansion which once stood there built by a gentleman called Walker. He was no relation of the Yaralla Walkers who lived in the adjoining suburb of Concord.

Homebush

The land on the west side of Homebush Bay once belonged to D'Arcy Wentworth. Wentworth, born in Ireland in 1764, served as an apprentice surgeon in his country of birth before leaving for London to complete his studies. In England he was twice arrested for highway robbery and twice discharged for lack of evidence. To keep him out of trouble, friends arranged an appointment for him as assistant surgeon on the convict transport *Neptune* of the Second Fleet, which arrived in Sydney in June 1790. Applying to Phillip for a post as Government Medical Officer, he was accepted and sent in that position to Norfolk Island penal colony, where he remained for six years with his wife, Catherine Crawley, a convict woman he had met on board the *Neptune*. They had three children, including the eldest William Wentworth, born soon after their arrival at Norfolk Island and conceived on the voyage out from England.

When D'Arcy returned to Sydney in 1796 he was appointed resident medical officer at Parramatta and also later served as a magistrate. In 1806 D'Arcy received a land grant from Governor King of 920 acres on the west side of the closest bay on the harbour to Parramatta on which he built a house called 'Home Bush', presumably as an abbreviation of "Home-in-the-Bush". In his stables on the property he kept livestock imported from South Africa and India, on which he would ride to Parramatta or

Sydney as business demanded. In the first horse race held in Sydney at Hyde Park in October 1810, his son William won the race on one of his father's horses.

Newington

Adjoining D'Arcy's Homebush estate to the west was Newington, granted to a free settler John Blaxland who arrived in Sydney with his younger brother Gregory in 1805. They called their estate after their birthplace of Newington in Kent. At Newington in Sydney the Blaxlands employed 70 convicts in various industries. They built small dykes on the flats along their property for evaporating tidal salt water in pans, the salt from which they used in the production of salted beef which they sold to ships in Sydney and to the Government for the army; they produced tweed and blankets in a textile mill and collected and burnt shells for building lime. During this period John Blaxland described the road to Sydney 'not a

bridge had been built, with three rivers to cross, which could only be effected at low tide by getting out of the gig and stepping from stone to stone. The road, a cart track only the width of the wheels, the wild natural forest almost closing overhead, chill and silent, can never be forgotten.'

On 11 May 1813 William Wentworth set off on horseback with Gregory Blaxland, a former army officer William Lawson and four convict stockmen to search for a way across the Blue Mountains to the west, a barrier which had frustrated all previous attempts to cross it in the first twenty five years of settlement. Wentworth and his group successfully made the crossing on a route now followed by The Great Western Highway and railway, to their eternal glory and the eternal gratitude of Governor Macquarie, who rewarded them each with a land grant of 1,000 acres.

D'Arcy Wentworth was later appointed Superintendent of Police by Macquarie and founded Sydney's

first Police Force. He died at Homebush aged sixty-three in 1827. His house 'Homebush' didn't survive the years. It's ruins stood for a time on the site of the Homebush abattoirs.

A colonial style homestead completed by the Blaxlands in 1832 and a chapel, St Augustines, built for their private worship, are both still standing in Slough Avenue Silverwater. The Royal Australian Navy's Newington Armaments depot now occupies much of the former Blaxland estate.

Homebush Bicentennial Park

The Homebush Bicentennial Park on the south side of the bay, covering 100 hectares of which about 60 hectares are mangroves and salt-marsh, was a rubbish tip in 1983 when the Government embarked on an ambitious project to transform the derelict land into an open grassy landscaped park with lakes, trees, shrubs and barbecue and picnic areas criss-crossed by paths for walkers and cyclists.

The park can be explored with the help of a map available at the Visitor Centre. A boardwalk running through the grey mangroves is particularly worth a visit in Autumn when golden orb spiders weave a canopy of webs in the mangrove branches overhead. The surrounding mangrove flats are a refuge for waterbirds, and ducks, pelicans, terns, cormorants and sandpipers are just a few of the species that frequent the park at different times of the year. Points of interest in the park include displays and education facilities in the field study centre, a giant sundial, and the central "treillage" or

A harbour ferry (below) proceeds along the main channel of Sydney Harbour between Putney Park in the foreground and Wangal Centenary Bushland Reserve on Mortlake Point on the other side of the harbour. The last of Sydney's vehicle ferries operates between Putney Park and Mortlake Point. The site of a punt ferry service since 1896, the first cable ferry on the run powered by a steam winch was opened for service in 1927. In the background between Majors Bay on the left and Yaralla Bay on the right are the mansion and extensive grounds of the old Yaralla homestead.

viewing tower, with panoramic views of the park after an energetic climb to the top. From the Tea House it is approximately a 4 kilometre return walk to a small viewing tower close to the waterbird refuge at the northernmost point of the park. The Bicentennial Park was opened on January 1 1988 as a sister park to Centennial Park in the city opened exactly 100 years previously.

Bordering the Bicentennial Park is the State Sports Centre and the Olympic Pool, Olympic Stadium and other facilities for the 2000 Olympics, in preparation to stage the best Olympics the world has ever seen.

Concord.

On Christmas Eve 1793, acting Governor Francis Grose distributed ten land grants of 25 acres each to 6 non-commissioned officers of the New South Wales Corps and four free settlers along an area of waterfront on the harbour shore between present day Rhodes and Mortlake. Grose had served as an officer with the British Army in Massachusetts during the American War of Independence, and called the locality of the land grants 'Concord' after a town in Massachusetts named originally after the Quaker word for "brotherly love".

In 1797 Governor Hunter granted 50 acres in the area to an ex-convict,

Isaac Nichols, transported for stealing a donkey. Nichols called his estate 'Yaralla' after the aboriginal word for a camp, bought up adjoining lots and established fruit orchards on his holding. He later built a schooner, the *Governor Hunter*, which traded along the New South Wales coast, and went on to become Australia's first postmaster in Sydney in 1809. At about this time (1810), Macquarie described the Concord residents 'The settlers are very poor, and live in mean, dirty, small habitations'.

The Walkers

Nichols' heirs sold Yaralla to Thomas Walker in 1840. Walker was a Scot

'Yaralla' homestead (below) is now the
Dame Eadith Walker Convalescent
Hospital. Cows and horses graze in the
grounds of the enormous estate
surrounding the house.

ing by water to alight at the steps of a stone quay or by carriage through an entrance gate and along a long drive lined by brush box trees through the grounds. The most distinguished guests of the era stayed at the house, including the Prince of Wales in 1921 (later King Edward VIII) and the Duke of York (later King George VI).

From the vast fortune he accumulated Walker gave many anonymous donations to charities and distributed funds through trustees to orphans, widows and families in need. Walker had one daughter, Eadith, born when he was sixty five, who he left the bulk of his fortune to when he died in 1886. Much of the remainder of his estate went into a trust fund of £100,000 to build a convalescent hospital for women on the western peninsula of the Yaralla estate. Built in 'Queen Anne' style, designed by architect John Sulman, the hospital opened as the Thomas Walker Convalescent Home and received it's first patients in 1893.

Eadith was aged 21 when her father died and carried on his good works. During the First World War she offered part of the grounds of Yaralla to the Government as a hospital for returned servicemen. Today it is the Concord General Repatriation Hospital. For this and many other charitable works Eadith was made a Dame of the British Empire in 1929. When she died unmarried in 1937 aged 73, Eadith left Yaralla homestead and grounds as a convalescent hospital for men administered by the Royal Prince Alfred Hospital.

Yaralla is significant today as the only one of Sydney's grand harbourside mansions still surrounded by its own grounds stretching to the waterfront, even if the grounds themselves are but a pale imitation of their former glory.

A good walk which can be covered in sections or done in one go occupying the best part of a day, includes a stroll through the grounds of Yaralla (Now the Dame Eadith Walker

who had arrived in Sydney aged 18 in 1822 to join his uncle who was a senior partner in a company of merchants. Walker did exceptionally well in business, rising to the top of his uncle's company and establishing his own business interests in pastoral properties and shipping. For many years he was President of the Bank of New South Wales.

Walker engaged well-known Sydney architect Edmund Blackett (designer of St Andrews Cathedral and many other churches) to design a house on his land at Concord, who produced an Italianate style mansion with a square tower and wide verandahs. Stone for the house was quarried on the east side of the estate by

Italian artisans, who built a swimming pool in the quarry they created (now filled in) and laid out an exotic garden of paths lined with succulents, palms, bamboo and orchids sprouting from concrete grottoes. Above the gardens a balustraded terrace and lawns sloped up to the main house. Nearby in the grounds was a tennis court, the first squash court built in New South Wales and in an outhouse a diesel turbine to generate electricity. "Yaralla", as Thomas Walker called his mansion, was the first house to be lit by electricity in Sydney. In the late nineteenth and early twentieth century the house was the centre of Sydney society, the owners hosting many dinner parties and balls, with guests arriv-

Hospital) and the Thomas Walker Hospital. A key is available on paying a refundable deposit to Concord Council for access through some gates in the hospital grounds, though the walk can be completed without it by diverting around fences.

Start at the end of Regent Street in Putney, and follow Waterview Street to Bennelong Park. Walking through Bennelong Park, Kissing Point Park and around Kissing Point Bay (where the way isn't very clear but follow the shoreline), continue through Putney Park and catch the Mortlake vehicle ferry to Hilly Street Mortlake. Walk through the streets of Concord and through Majors Bay Reserve to the gate at the entrance to Yaralla. The path follows the foreshore through the grounds of Yaralla and Concord Repatriation Hospital on Yaralla Bay to the Thomas Walker Hospital. There's a most impressive vista of the north elevation of the Queen Anne facade of the hospital from a boathouse on the harbour. Continue

around Brays Bay (named after John Bray, the first of the original ten settlers to build a house on his grant) on a boardwalk through the mangroves in Rhodes Park, then through McIlwaine Park to Concord Road at Llewellyn Street. Cross the harbour on the Ryde Road Bridge and return to Waterview Street via Riverside Avenue and Osborne Avenue

Mortlake

Breakfast Point Mortlake is 250 metres across the Harbour from Raven Point Tennyson. On 5 February 1788 a boat party with Captain Hunter and Lieutenant Bradley on board left Cockatoo Island where they had spent the previous night, rowed 5 kilometres to present day Mortlake and cooked their breakfast on the shore. The spot where they landed was marked Breakfast Point on Hunter's first map of the Harbour. Seeing some aborigines on the north shore of the Harbour, the men of Hunter's party

'made signs to them to come over and waved green boughs'. Seven aborigines crossed the Harbour, left their spears in their dug-out canoes, and accepted gifts of beads from the whitemen.

The Australian Gas Light Company's works occupying 100 acres on the waterfront at Mortlake were one of the world's biggest gas works during the time they operated from 1886 to 1976. The works burned 450,000 tons of coal a year in the pro-

The jetty and swimming pool of Cabarita Park are visible in the foreground of this view of the Parramatta River. On the right above the swimming pool are in sequence, the opening of Hen and Chicken Bay, the suburb of Abbotsford, Abbotsford Bay, the suburb of Chiswick, and the opening of Five Dock Bay. On the left are Looking Glass Point, Looking Glass Bay, Bedlam Point, the suburb of Henley and the Gladesville Bridge.

duction of gas, brought directly to a wharf on the Harbour by colliers making the journey from Newcastle on the Hunter Valley. When Sydney was converted to natural gas the Mortlake works closed, and today the retorts and other facilities of the works stand quietly like massive sculptures by the harbour fore-shore. Natural gas from Moomba central Australia is piped directly to Mortlake where it is reticulated through the original coal gas mains.

Cabarita Park, across Kendall Bay from the old gasworks, is named after the Aboriginal word for 'by the water'. A monument in the park pays tribute to William Beach, 'undefeated

From left to right (below) France Bay, Canada Bay and Exile Bay on Hen and Chicken Bay. On the right on Exile Bay is Massey Park Public Golf Course.

champion sculler of the world' for three years from 1884 to 1887 when he retired aged 37. A crowd estimated at 100,000 crowded the headlands along the Parramatta River course including Cabarita Point, to watch Beach defeat the Canadian Ted Hanlan for the world championship on 16 August 1884. On 1st of January 1901 the birth of the Federation of Australia was proclaimed by the First Governor General, the Earl of Hopetoun from a pavilion in Centennial Park Sydney. Exactly fifty years later in 1951 the pavilion was moved from Centennial Park to Cabarita Park where it still stands today.

Hen and Chicken Bay

The eastern shore of Cabarita Park is washed by the waters of Hen and Chicken Bay, an irregular indentation on the Harbour nearly 3 kilometres long and an average of 750 metres wide, with three small bays along it's western shore. The first foot

track to Parramatta skirted the mud-flats at the southern end of the bay. The distance from Sydney to Parramatta was 22 kilometres, more than could be comfortably covered in a day by soldiers escorting convicts. A stockade was built as an overnight guardhouse at the halfway mark close to the flats at the head of Hen and Chicken Bay called The Long Bottom or 'long swamp' after the old English word of 'bottom' for low-lying land or swamp.

In 1837, rebellions against British rule in Canada were crushed by a military force commanded by Sir George Arthur, a former Governor of Van Diemen's Land (Tasmania). Twenty nine of the rebels were executed and 149 others, who became known as the "Canadian Exiles", were transported for life to Australia. Fifty eight French Canadians arrived in Sydney on 25th February 1840 and were confined by the Governor Sir George Gipps in the Long Bottom Stockade. The prisoners were treated more leniently than

The shipyards and workshops at Cockatoo Island (above) were once the biggest industrial establishment in Australia. The Sutherland and Fitzroy dry docks, excavated in the nineteenth century, are on the right side of the Island. To the right of and behind the chimney are some of the Island's original sandstone buildings built by convict labour. Many of the workshops on the island have been demolished since the shipyards closed in the 1980's.

Wrights Point Drummoyne (left) with Five Dock Bay in the background. At the tip of Wrights Point are the stone landing steps of the original Drummoyne House.

other convicts, worked on the Long Bottom Farm and on the Parramatta Road and were allowed a certain degree of freedom, spending some of their time around the shores of Hen and Chicken Bay. In 1844 the 'Exiles' received full pardons. Two of the original fifty eight had died in Sydney, one married an Australian girl and settled here and the other fifty five returned to Canada. Their memory lingers in the names of Canada Bay, Exile Bay and France Bay on the west side of Hen and Chicken Bay.

Five Dock

In 1790 the Irish Surgeon John Harris arrived in Sydney on the Second Fleet with the posting of Medical Officer to the British garrison. Harris was granted 750 acres of land in 1806 by governor King, comprising the entire peninsula between Hen and Chicken Bay and Iron Cove. Harris called his property 'Five Dock Farm' after an unusual formation of five short fingers of rock projecting into the harbour like "five docks" on present day

Five Dock Point. Two of the 'docks' were later covered by the southern abutment of the first Gladesville Bridge.

In 1826 a track was cut through the bush from Parramatta Road through Harris' property to a point where the harbour channel is only 250 metres wide in present day Abbotsford for 'The Great North Road' connecting Sydney with the settlements of the Hawkesbury and Hunter valleys. A punt ferry went into service on the crossing, operated by a winch and cable, the first ferry on the Harbour that could carry a horse and cart.

Harris sold Five Dock Farm in 1836 to a former convict, Samuel Lyons for £8000 and died just two years later aged 82, unmarried, with no heirs and one of the richest men in Sydney. Lyons sub-divided his holding into 133 lots, of sizes from 1 to 28 hectares, many of them with water frontages and advertised in the Australian on January 24 1837, proclaiming the land offered, 'repose after the anxiety

of business' in 'beauty of scenery wholly unmatched in New South Wales.'

In 1921 the author and poet Henry Lawson rented a cottage on the Great North Road where he spent the last eight months of his life, living alone, writing a novel *Deadly in Earnest and Casually Australian*. The novel was uncompleted when he died. Henry Lawson Avenue turning west off The Great North Road in Abbotsford is named after him.

Abbotsford House, a mansion on the west side of Abbotsford Bay, was built in 1878 by Sir Arthur Renwick, a politician and philanthropist. The house stands today in the grounds of the old Nestles factory.

Part of Harris' estate was bought by a wealthy shipowner, William Wright. In 1854 Wright built a large house overlooking the Harbour called 'Drummoyne', or 'flat topped ridge', after the Gaelic words 'drum' (ridge) and 'moyne' (flat or plain). Not long before building the house, Wright had contracted to supply the carriages for the first railway line in Australia between Sydney and Parramatta through a company belonging to one of his relatives, Wright & Co Birmingham England. The original Drummoyne House was demolished, but the stone landing stage with broad stone steps and carved stone balustrades remains as a landmark at Wrights Point on the Harbour.

Gladesville Bridge

In 1881 work started on the construction of a swing bridge from Five Dock Point to Gladesville. Opened in 1884, the Bridge was the first across the main channel of Sydney Harbour. With the opening of the Bridge the punt operating between Abbotsford and Bedlam Point was taken out of service and ever since 'The Great North Road' has been a road to nowhere. On 2 October 1964 the massive concrete span of the new Gladesville Bridge opened, spanning the Harbour at a site 250 metres east of the old bridge. The new Bridge, with a span of 1,000 feet and a clearance for shipping of 134 feet at high tide, was the longest concrete arch bridge in the world when it opened. In 1979 it was outstripped by a concrete bridge in Yugoslavia 300 feet longer.

Cockatoo Island

Cockatoo Island off the shore of Drummoyne, covering 40 acres, is the largest island on Sydney Harbour. It was named after the numerous white cockatoos that flocked to the branches of the giant red gum trees that originally covered the Island.

Cockatoo Island remained uninhabited until the end of 1838 when convicts were moved from Goat Island to build grain stores. Twenty grain stores twenty feet deep were chiselled out from solid sandstone on the crown of the Island 'in the shape of bottles' and remained in use for many years as government grain stores. Following the end of convict transportation by Britain in 1840 Cockatoo Island was made a New South Wales penal establishment and prisoners were set to work constructing a gaol for themselves from sandstone blocks and quarrying stone for the work at 'Semi-Circular-Quay'. In 1851 prisoners started the mammoth task of excavating by hand from solid sandstone a large graving dock on the east of the island for use by the British navy. Called the Fitzroy Dock after Sir Charles Fitzroy, Governor of NSW 1846-55, it was first used in 1857.

On 11 September 1863, Frederick Ward, an Australian born bushranger sentenced to life imprisonment for stealing cattle, escaped from Cockatoo Island by swimming across the channel to the harbour shore. Ward or "Captain Thunderbolt" as he was better known, continued his bushranging activities on the northern tablelands of New South Wales for six years until he was shot dead by police in May 1870.

When the Island was closed as a prison in 1871 the buildings were used as a reformatory for female prisoners and juvenile delinquents until 1908.

From the 1870's to the 1960's Cockatoo Island was one of the biggest shipyards and naval dockyards in Australia. During the First World War four destroyers and two light cruisers were built there. At the peak of activity in the Second World War, 3,600 men were engaged in the workshops of Cockatoo Island on naval shipbuilding and repair, including conversion of merchant ships to troop transports, hospital ships and auxiliary cruisers.

One of the last merchant ships built there, the 9,850 ton car ferry *Empress of Australia* launched in 1965, was used on the Melbourne to Hobart route for many years. After being sold later to overseas owners she sank in the Malacca Straight in 1992 after colliding with another ship. A destroyer built at Cockatoo, The *HMAS Vampire*, is now a floating exhibit at the National Maritime Museum, Darling Harbour.

These days Cockatoo Island is uninhabited and silent once more following the closure of the workshops and dockyard and awaits a decision as to it's future role.

Iron Cove

Iron Cove on the east side of the Drummoyne peninsula, 2.5 kilometres long and an average of 500 metres wide, is thought to have been named after the ironbark trees which once lined it's banks. When struck with the axes carried by the early settlers it was just as likely for a piece to break off the axe than to make an impression on the 'iron' trunk of the tree.

In 1844 a boiling down plant established by Charles Abercrombie had its works at the north-west point of the Cove, where by-products from the slaughter house were "boiled down" for glue, tallow and hides. After buying up properties adjoining his works, in 1855 Abercrombie was offering 'highly valuable waterside allotments' on his 'Birkenhead Estate', named after the Merseyside town in England.

In 1899 Henry Perdriau built the Perdriau Rubber Factory on a large site on the north west side of the bay. Among the wide range of rubber products produced were mackintoshes, rubber dolls, galoshes and tyres. The company was bought out by Dunlop in 1928, who continued production there until closing the works down in 1977, when the Birkenhead Point shopping complex was created on the site occupying the former rubber company buildings.

Rodd Island

From Brett Park Drummoyne a circular two hour 7 kilometre walk follows the shore of the Cove. Starting at the car park at Brett Park near the west end of the Iron Cove Bridge, follow Henley Marine Drive to Rodd Point, a pleasant grassy knoll projecting from the shore into the waters of Iron Cove. On the Point are picnic facilities and the Rodd Family mausoleum crowned by a stone cross. Both the cross and the mausoleum were carved out of the solid rock of the Point by convicts in the nineteenth century. Brent Rodd, a solicitor, bought a section of waterfront land including Rodd Point from the Five Dock Estate in 1838, and built a large house called Barnstaple Manor which stood nearby on present day Princess Avenue.

Rodd Island, 250 metres away on the Cove, has had a varied history as a bacteriological station, a park, and a training base for U.S. troops during the Second World War. In the 1880's a 'Rabbit Commission' was established by the New South Wales Government to investigate ways of eradicating the rabbit plague that was then wreaking destruction throughout the arable lands of New South Wales. The Government offered a reward of £25,000 to anyone who could develop a method of ending the rabbit menace and resumed Rodd Island for use as a bacteriological laboratory, where scientists sent out by Louis Pasteur led by Dr Adrien Loire carried out experiments using Pasteur's chicken cholera microbe. Loire announced they'd discovered a way to eradicate the rabbits, and claimed the reward, but the microbe they developed also killed native birdlife and the New South Wales Government refused to pay.

While Loire was working at the Island the French actress Sarah Bernhardt arrived in Sydney for a tour of Australia. The actress was dismayed to discover that two pet dogs accompanying her would have to be quarantined during her stay. Dr Loire chivalrously came to her rescue by offering to look after the dogs on Rodd Island, which the New South Wales Government specially gazetted as an animal quarantine station. Loire became great friends with Sarah Bernhardt who gave him walk-on rolls in some of her plays.

In 1859 Brent Rodd had made a down-payment on the Island, and named it after himself, but much to his fury the deposit was later rescinded and the Island turned instead for a time into a public reserve. These days the Island is a public reserve once more. Intending visitors should first seek permission from the National Parks and Wildlife Service. The building used by Loire for his experiments is still on the Island.

Continuing south on Henley Marine Drive, follow Dobroyd Parade past Haberfield Rowing Club to Leichardt Park. From the park the walk continues along the shore through the grounds of Rozelle Hospital. The hospital buildings, designed in 1878 by Government Architect James Barnett as the 'Callan Park Hospital for the Insane' are one of the most significant and intact collections of sandstone buildings built in the Victorian period in Sydney. Walk through King George Park and across Manning Street to Clubb Street to cross the Iron Bridge on the pedestrian footway and return to Brett Park.

Balmain

The Scotsman William Balmain was 26 when he arrived in Sydney with the First Fleet as naval surgeon on board the convict transport *Alexander*. After serving as a medical officer in Sydney, (he had exhibited 'great skill' in operating on Governor Phillip to remove the spear shaft after the Governor was speared by an aborigine at Collins Beach), then as medical superintendent on Norfolk Island, he returned to Sydney in 1795 and was promoted to chief medical officer of New South Wales and was also later appointed a magistrate.

Balmain received land grants of 270 acres at Windsor, 425 acres in The Field of Mars in present day Ryde and on 26 April 1800, 550 acres from Governor Hunter comprising almost the entire northern section of the peninsula between Iron Cove and Darling Harbour at present day Balmain. William Balmain had been involved in private trading as a merchant, importing rum and tea from India, however in September 1800, when Governor King succeeded Hunter as Governor, he issued an immediate decree banning trading by

colonial officials. Balmain left Sydney for England in August 1801, but the month before his departure sold his 550 acre land grant on Darling Harbour to a Calcutta merchant, John Gilchrist for 5 shillings, a low price which is assumed to have been an ex-gratia payment for a previous or future consignment of goods. After reaching England Balmain died in London just two years later in 1803 as a 41 year old bachelor, leaving his remaining Sydney estates to an illegitimate son and daughter in Sydney.

John Gilchrist settled in Sydney as a merchant and shipowner and during the term of office of Governor Darling (1825-31) built a road branching off the Parramatta Road near Leichardt through to the eastern tip of 'Balmain's Grant'. The portion of the road through his property was named 'Gilchrist Place' (later changed to Darling Road) and the section from Parramatta Road to 'Balmain's Grant' was called Balmain Road. Gilchrist then subdivided and

Birkenhead Point Shops and Marina (below) with the Iron Cove Bridge and Iron Cove in the background. Cabin cruisers and small runabouts are available on hire from the Marina.

Longnose Point at Birchgrove (right). On the shore between the Point and Iron Cove Bridge is the Dawn Fraser Swimming Pool and Elkington Park.

The ferry repair and service depot on Mort Bay, Balmain (below right). In the background are Johnstons Bay and White Bay and the Bulk Wheat Terminal and grain silos of Glebe Island.

sold the land, the first lots going for £56 each in 1836. Eventually taking a profit of £50,000 on the land sales, Gilchrist's enterprise entered Sydney folklore to describe someone who has done well in business with the expression "has bought all Balmain for five bob and sold it for a quid."

Thomas Sutcliffe Mort from Lancashire in England arrived in Sydney aged 22 in 1838, worked as a wool buyer, then made a fortune after becoming a wool broker in 1843. Mail steamers had started arriving in Australia in 1852, but no dry dock was available in Sydney to accommodate them. Mort bought ten acres of land in Balmain in 1854 and using a gang of returned prospectors from the goldfields working with picks and shovels excavated a dry dock 400 feet long by 50 feet wide out of solid sandstone. Business expanded into engineering and shipbuilding, including the construction of coastal steamers and locally built steam locomotives. When formed into a public company in 1872 the 'Mort's Dock and Engineering Company' was the largest industrial company in Australia. Mort also pioneered the use of refrigeration in ships for the export from Australia of refrigerated beef and mutton. From the 38,000 acre estate Mort owned at Bodalla on the south coast, he established a cheesemaking factory which still markets cheese to this day. The Mort's Dockyard waterfront properties were sold when the company went into liquidation in 1959. Mort Bay Park on Mort Bay, is on the site of the former works.

Balmain Coal Mine

Sydney sits on top of the centre of one of the biggest deposits of black coal in the world, covering 50,000 square kilometres. Since the early days of settlement coal had been mined on the northern rim of the deposit at Newcastle, west of the Blue Mountains at Lithgow and on the southern rim of the deposit at Wollongong. The presence of coal below Sydney was confirmed at various sites at the end of the nineteenth

century using diamond drill test bores and in June 1897 Sydney Harbour Collieries Ltd started sinking the 'Jubillee' (named after Queen Victoria's Diamond Jubilee) and 'Birthday' shafts on the Harbour at Balmain on a site now owned by Howard Smith Industries next to Birchgrove Primary School. The shafts, each 18 feet wide, 2,784 feet deep and lined by over 4 million bricks, took five years to sink and were the second deepest in the world at the time.

An underground galley over a mile long extended from the bottom of the shaft, to a point approximately below Simmons Point Balmain, along which the coal was transported after being extracted from an area beneath the Harbour between Balmain and Balls Head.

A miner described conditions at the mine in the Labour Daily in 1924: 'The cage in which we go down this deep shaft appears to have outlived its usefulness. Some of the side plates are eaten through with rust. It is still used for lowering and raising men - thirty six at a time. When we step on the cage to go into this living tomb, we do not know but that the day may be our last... A few yards from the shaft bottom we have several minutes to get our eyes accustomed to the dungeon-like darkness of our surroundings. Then we start in single file - a stream of men about seventy in number. The dust begins to rise from under our feet and we are in a cloud due to horse refuse and stone dust... After the best part of an hour's walk under beautiful Sydney Harbour, we reach, in a half dazed state, the coal face...'

Coal was mined during two periods from 1902-15, and again from 1924-31. The workings were never economic and the value of the coal extracted didn't cover the enormous capital cost of sinking the shafts. When the mine closed the shafts were filled with fly ash from the White Bay Power Station, and the shaft heads sealed with concrete in 1957.

Mort Bay at the lower centre of the picture above is enclosed by Ballast Point on the left and the peninsular of East Balmain on the right. Mort Bay Park at the lower right of the picture was once the Mort Company dry dock, workshops and shipbuilding yard.

John Birch, paymaster of Macquarie's 73rd regiment, bought land at the northern tip of Balmain in 1810. The orchard he established there he called Birch Grove and his house, the first in the area, he named Birch Grove House. The reserve close to the ferry wharf on Long Nose Point at Birchgrove was the site of the

Morrison Sinclair shipyards, which were resumed for conversion to a park in the 1970's.

On the harbour not far west of the site of the old coal mine is the Dawn Fraser Swimming Pool, renamed from the Elkington Park Baths in 1964 to honour Balmain born Dawn Fraser, winner of the woman's 100 metres free style at three consecutive Olympic Games, Melbourne in 1956, Rome in 1960 and Tokyo in 1964. The pool, dating back to 1881, is located next to the grass, flower-beds and palm trees of Elkington Park.

Some of the best late-colonial period buildings built in Sydney are located in Balmain, in particular the com-

plex of James Barnett's Courthouse, Town Hall and Post Office on Darling Street. Also on Darling Street is one of the oldest houses in Balmain, the Waterman's Cottage at number 12, built by a Scottish stonemason John Cavill in 1841.

Balmain used to be a working class industrial suburb, many of the residents working at Mort's docks and railway workshops, the coal mine, or the coal burning power stations at Rozelle or White Bay. All these industries are now closed and Balmain has recently changed it's image into a sought after residential suburb within convenient reach of the city. Ferries from Darling Street Wharf at Balmain take only a few minutes to commute to Circular Quay or to the ferry wharf at Sydney Aquarium in Darling Harbour, ten minutes walk from Martin Place and the city centre.

Industry has remained on the south east shore of Balmain at the White Bay container terminals. White Bay was named after Balmain's predecessor in the post of Senior Medical Officer, Surgeon John White, who arrived in Sydney with Balmain on the First Fleet and held the post from 1788 until returning to England in 1794.

Annandale

Neighbouring Annandale was named by Major George Johnson of the First Fleet after his birthplace of Annandale in Scotland. Phillip made Johnson a commander of a company of the New South Wales Corps in 1792 and granted him 100 acres of land on the Parramatta Road where he built 'Annandale House'. On 26th January 1808, the 20th anniversary of settlement at Sydney Cove, Johnson, now in full command of the New South Wales Corps, led the troops which overthrew Governor Bligh in the Rum Rebellion. Johnson had hatched the plot to overthrow Bligh from Annandale House. Recalled to England in 1809 to face a court-martial for mutiny and sailing back on the same ship as Governor Bligh, Johnson was found guilty and cashiered, but returned to Sydney in 1813, where he found favour with Macquarie. He lived at Annandale House with his convict wife Esther and their three sons and two daughters and died there in January 1823 aged 58. The entrance gates of Annandale House are now in the grounds of Annandale Public School on Johnson Street.

Glebe

The adjoining suburb of Glebe is on the harbour frontage of Blackwattle Bay and Rozelle Bay. In August 1789 Governor Phillip made a 400 acre land grant in the area to the chaplain of the First Fleet the Reverend Richard Johnson for use as 'church land or glebe'. Glebe in Ecclesiastical Law is 'land devoted to the maintenance of the incumbent of the Church'. That land was later parcelled out to officers and Johnson accepted an alternative grant of land further south in what is now known as the Sydney suburb of Canterbury.

A large area of parkland has been created on Rozelle Bay at the end of Glebe Point Road with the Pope Paul VI Park and adjoining Glebe Bicentennial Park. The Sydney Fish Markets, accessible from Pyrmont Bridge Road on Blackwattle Bay, are the best location in Sydney for a choice of fresh reasonably priced seafood.

Glebe Island on Victoria Road, now joined to the mainland, is occupied by massive grain silos and specialises in the handling of wheat and flour for export. A monument on Glebe Island commemorates the arrival of the first U.S. soldiers in Sydney on 28th of March 1942 on board the Queen Mary. The liner anchored in Athol Bay close to Taronga Zoo and the 8,398 troops on board were taken on harbour ferries to Glebe Island, where troop trains took them to camps outside the city. Glebe Island remained the main base in Sydney during the war for the embarking and re-embarking of American troops and for the handling and storage of American supplies for the war effort.

Pyrmont

Pyrmont is another industrial suburb which is currently undergoing a transformation as the industries such as the Pyrmont Power Station, wheat silos and flour mills, meat cold stores and cargo wharves are closed down and replaced by housing and apartments, parks and the Sydney Casino. One industry that is likely to remain for a time is The Colonial Sugar Refining Company on Johnstons Bay, better known these days as "C.S.R.' who established a sugar refinery on the west side of Pyrmont in 1878. Extensively enlarged since then and now one of the biggest industrial establishments on the Harbour, the factory produces among other products large quantities of industrial alcohol distilled from sugar.

Cargo wharves at berths 12, 13 and 14 Pyrmont were used during the Second World War for the embarkation of Australian soldiers and the shipping of war materials. A memorial plaque at the site is a reminder of those who never returned.

Pyrmont itself was originally a land grant to John Macarthur of Parramatta merino wool fame, and a co-conspirator with Johnson in the overthrow of Governor Bligh. According to a December 1806 copy of the Sydney Gazette, the suburb received it's name when 21 ladies and gentlemen made an 'aquatic excursion from Parramatta to Captain Macarthur's estate at Cockle Bay', where they enjoyed a picnic 'beneath the shelter of a spreading fig tree.' Admiring the 'romantic scene' with its 'picturesque beaches...one of the young ladies was pleased to give the name of Pyrmont, from the pure and uncontaminated spring, joined to the native beauties of the place' after the medicinal springs of Pyrmont near Hanover in Germany.

Darling Harbour

Darling Harbour's deepwater anchorages were not developed in the first 22 years of white settlement because the ridge between it and Sydney Cove was too steep for cart traffic. Instead, its shores were convenient places to collect reeds for roof thatch and to catch a side dish of molluscs the Aborigines called "pipis" and the English called "cockles". So it was long known as Cockle Bay until renamed in honour of Governor Darling during his term in office between 1825 and 1831.

Darling Harbour developed as wharves and an industrial area following the opening of the first steam

mill there in 1815, kick starting Australia's industrial age and quickly replacing the windmills on the heights around Sydney. Industries associated with saw milling, ship building, soap manufacture and meat processing quickly followed, and the swamps at the head of the bay were filled in to create a giant railway goods yard. With the transformation of cargo handling by the advent of the container and an increasing reliance on road transport in the 1970's, the Darling Harbour railway yards became disused. So in the 1980's a consortium of government and private enterprise transformed the 54 hectare site with Australia's most ambitious urban redevelopment project to produce a new Darling Harbour for the people.

There are many elements to the new Darling Harbour and there is a strongly utilitarian aspect to them all.

On the west side of Cockle Bay is the Australian National Maritime Museum.

The Exhibition Centre, which has a column free indoor area the size of five football fields, was sorely needed for trade shows and public displays. And the neighbouring Darling Harbour Convention Centre can seat 3,500 delegates, making it the largest such venue in Australia.

There is an appealing concentration of museums and other public entertainment complexes. The Entertainment Centre straddles the division between Darling Harbour and Chinatown. Many of the world's biggest stars have performed at the "Ent Cent" and many more will probably do so - as long as Sydney's summer is contemporaneous with northern winters.

A closer cultural link is forged by the Chinese Garden built as a bicentennial gift by the government of China's Guangdong Province. Within the walls is a peaceful garden refuge of lakes, waterfalls and ingeniously executed landscaping.

Tumbalong Park is a grassy circle fringed by eucalyptus trees, with tree-lined paths radiating into the middle distance. Catering for playtime for all ages there is both a children's play ground and amphitheatre for open air performances. The emphasis in the park is on Australian vegetation - the first greening of Darling Harbour since the last reeds were cut.

The Powerhouse Museum started life as the power plant for Sydney's trams and has ended up as a celebration of arts, technology and social history. It's big enough to contain the whole Opera House and the daunted visitor may feel, that must be about the only object not on display.

The Sydney Aquarium, on the city side of the water's edge and shaped like a breaking wave, contains a good cross section of the incredible range of fish that inhabit Australian waters. Sydney's sharks can be confronted in nose-to-nose meetings in the aquarium's transparent tunnel.

———————————————

Rozelle Bay and Blackwattle Bay (above left) with Pyrmont, Darling Harbour and the City in the background.

Darling Harbour (above), with Sydney Aquarium on the left and in sequence from the foreground on the right, the National Maritime Museum, Harbourside Festival Markets, Sydney Convention Centre and Sydney Exhibition Centre.

THE ROCKS TO DOUBLE BAY

Exclusive suburbs and Sydney's birthplace

Stroll the historic Rocks area and bustling Circular Quay. See Sydney's incomparable Opera House and wander the beautiful Royal Botanic Gardens. Visit elegant Elizabeth Bay House and the harbourside suburbs of Darling Point and Double Bay.

The highground of Millers Point on the east side of Darling Harbour is named after an ex-convict John Leighton, better known as "Jack the Miller", who operated three windmills on the point in the early nineteenth century. One night in 1826 Leighton, known as 'a jovial though somewhat frugal man', got drunk, slipped climbing the steps of one of his windmills and tumbled to his death.

The old stone quay and warehouse of Moore's Wharf constructed on the north side of the Point in 1835, was the point of export from Sydney of much of the gold won from the gold-fields during the 1850's. In 1855 the first steam trains to arrive in Australia were landed at the wharf and hauled up the steep incline of Millers Point on their way to Redfern Station.

The Rocks

The Rocks, on the east side of the approach to the Harbour Bridge, was a region named by the first settlers after the rocky ridge that ran north-south along the point. When David Collins of the First Fleet first stepped ashore on the west side of Sydney Cove, it was 'from the boat literally into a wood', onto a shore lined by the rocks of 'long sandstone ledges and lintels'.

The southern pylons of the Harbour Bridge rest on the shore of Dawes Point, named after Lieutenant William Dawes, astronomer with the First Fleet. Within a few days of his arrival Dawes had erected a hut on the point to house his telescope and other instruments, to observe the transit through the southern skies of 'Maskelyne's Comet' due to be visible in Sydney later in 1788. He was a man who, according later to Mrs Elizabeth Macarthur of Elizabeth Farm Parramatta was 'so much engaged with the stars that, to mortal eyes he is not always visible'. Dawes supervised the construction in November 1788 of an earthen redoubt mounted with 8 guns from The Sirius. 'Dawes Battery' as the position became known was later built into a permanent defensive position mounting five mortars, thirteen 42 pounders, a magazine, soldier's quarters and a residence for the C.O. The entire fort was demolished during the construction of the Harbour Bridge, but five cannon on carriages remain in Dawes Point Park below the south approach to the Harbour Bridge.

A palm tree-studded reserve on the Harbour across Hickson Road from Dawes Point Park has a superb view looking across the cove to the magnificent sails of Sydney Opera House. From the park a broad wooden boardwalk follows the waterline past one of Sydney's most exclusive hotels, the Park Hyatt Sydney, to Campbell's Storehouse on Campbell's Cove.

Campbells Store

The Scotsman Robert Campbell arrived in Sydney in 1798 from Calcutta with a shipload of general stores. He established the first private wharf and stores in Sydney, and became a wealthy merchant dealing in the import of rum and export of whale products, seal skins and wool. In 1801 he married Sophia Palmer, daughter of Commissary General John Palmer in charge of all Government stores. Campbell died at his country estate of Duntroon near Canberra (his house is now part of an army training college) and was buried at St John's church Canberra. The ground floor of the stores is now occupied by several good restaurants.

Sydney Cove Passenger Terminal on the west side of Sydney Cove was the point of disembarkation in Australia for hundreds of thousands of European migrants in the 1950's and 1960's. The terminal is still the point of call in Sydney for the world's great ocean liners such as the "QE2", the "Crystal Harmony" and the "Canberra". Behind the terminal is Cadman's Cottage, built in 1816, the oldest house in Sydney.

Occupying the old Maritime Services Board building south of the terminal is the Museum of Contemporary Art. The 'Stalinist' style of the exterior and the internal 1930's art-deco design could be considered a work of contemporary art in itself.

Circular Quay

Today's bustling scene at Circular Quay, is completely in contrast to that discovered by Governor Phillip little more than 200 years ago, when he chose Sydney as the site of a settlement because of the stream of fresh water running into the cove and the deep water anchorages close to the shore. When the first convicts with their guard of marines landed at Sydney Cove on the 27th of January 1788 to make a clearing, build huts and pitch tents, David Collins wrote in his journal '...the run of fresh water stole silently along through a very thick wood, the stillness of which had then, for the first time since the creation, been interrupted by the rude sound of the labourer's axe... a stillness and tranquillity which from that day were to give place to the voice of labour, the confusion of camps and towns and the busy hum of its new possessors'.

While the work continued of unloading stores and provisions and establishing the rudiments of a settlement, the women and children were kept on board the transports on Sydney Cove, until they were rowed ashore in longboats on the morning of 6 February. As Arthur Smyth, surgeon on the transport Lady Penrhyn later wrote, 'The men convicts got to the women very soon after they were landed, & it is beyond my abilities to give a just description of the scene of debauchery & riot that ensued during the night'. The debauchery continued into the night until a sudden ferocious thunderstorm with torrential rain swept the settlement and a bolt of lightening split a tree from top to bottom in the centre of the camp, killing five sheep and a hog. The following morning Phillip assembled

the convicts and warned them that the sentry had orders to fire with ball at any man seen in the women's camp after dark and all men practicing promiscuous intercourse could expect severe punishment.

Sydney Opera House
North of Circular Quay at Bennelong Point the great white shells of Sydney

Previous pages: Sydney Harbour Bridge and eastern Sydney Harbour, with the Opera House and Sydney's Eastern Suburbs on the right.

The Queen of the seas the 'QE 2' berths at Sydney Cove Passenger Terminal in The Rocks (below).

P & O's majestic 'Canberra' berthed at Sydney Cove Passenger Terminal at Circular Quay makes a fitting companion to Sydney Opera House on the opposite side of the Quay (far right).

The Park Hyatt Hotel and Campbell's Storehouse on Campbells Cove in The Rocks (right).

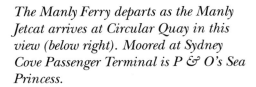

The Manly Ferry departs as the Manly Jetcat arrives at Circular Quay in this view (below right). Moored at Sydney Cove Passenger Terminal is P & O's Sea Princess.

Opera House rise from the Harbour like the hind quarters of a pair of giant white crayfish that have emerged from the water and been beached on the shore. The point was originally an island, known as 'Cattle Point' where the livestock from the First Fleet were unloaded then was renamed Bennelong Point after Bennelong the Aborigine, who lived there for a time in a small hut. A fort built by Macquarie occupied the site from 1821 to 1900, then a tram depot from 1902 to 1958, which was demolished to make way for the Opera House

The story of Sydney Opera House is a drama in itself.

The English composer Eugene Goosens, a direct descendant of Captain Cook, was appointed conductor of the Sydney Symphony Orchestra in 1947. Goossens persuaded the Labour Government of the day that Sydney should have its own Opera House for concerts and opera, and that it should be built on

Bennelong Point opposite the Harbour Bridge. In March 1956, the year following the announcement by the Government of Bennelong Point as the site for an Opera House, Goossens luggage was searched by customs at the airport when he was returning from a conducting tour overseas and found to contain a quantity of pornographic photos, films and books. Tried and found guilty of importing 'indecent material', Goossens resigned as conductor and left Australia that May.

An international design competition for a 'National Opera House', commissioned by the New South Wales Government in 1957 with a first prize of £5,000, received 233 entries and was won by the unanimous choice of the four judges by 38 year old Danish architect Jorn Utzon. A team of quantity surveyors examined the top ten designs from the competition and calculated that Utzon's plan would cost about 7 million dollars to build, the cheapest they thought, out of the ten they'd looked at. The government announced the Opera House would take three and a half years to complete.

To finance the project, a public lottery 'The Opera House Lottery' was started. Tragedy struck when following the publicity surrounding the awarding of one of the first prizes of £100.000, the winner's son, eight year old Graeme Thorne, was kidnapped, held to ransom, then murdered after the ransom was paid.

Construction of the Opera House proceeded slowly, largely due to design and construction difficulties associated with the unique architecture of the project. In February 1966, with construction still proceeding on the Opera House shells, Utzon resigned following disagreements with Davis Hughes, the Minister for Public Works in a new liberal state government. Pressured for completed working drawings of the interiors and with arguments raging over payment of fees and the structural feasibility of the ceilings of the theatres, Utzon wrote in his letter of resignation '...there has been no collaboration on the most vital items of the job in the last many months from your department's side.' Talking of 'malice in Blunderland' and later saying 'I do not care if they pull the Opera House down', Utzon asked that his name should no longer be associated with the project.

Utzon's design for the interior of the Opera House was shelved (the architect had completed virtually no drawings), and the design of the interior and the completion of the project was overseen by a team of four Australian architects, with Peter Hall as design architect.

One of the first decisions of the new architects, with the support of the New South Wales Government, was to change the major hall of the Opera House - against fierce public opposition - from a dual purpose hall for opera and concerts to a single

Sydney Royal Botanic Gardens and the City (top).

Fort Denison (above) during Sydney's Bicentenary celebrations in 1988.

purpose concert hall. Opera was relegated to what had been intended as a drama theatre in the minor hall, which in some respects was even less suitable for opera than some of the existing theatres in the city.

By the time the Opera House was officially opened by the Queen on Saturday October 20 1973 fifteen years after construction had started, the final cost of the project had increased to a mammoth 102 million. Jorn Utzon declined his invitation to attend the opening, and to date has never returned to Australia to see his completed masterpiece.

The years following the completion of the Opera House have proved it's success, not only as a design exercise, but as a performance venue. The acoustics of the Concert Hall are rated among the top three theatres in the world, while the complex of five theatres at the opera House is one of the busiest performing arts centres in the world, with an average of over 2,900 events held every year, from

open-air concerts to conventions and grand opera - held very successfully with the use of clever set design in the Concert Hall!

Farm Cove

East of the Opera House on Farm Cove the site of the Royal Botanic Gardens was the first area in Sydney to be successfully cultivated by the men of the First Fleet. By July 1788 a Government Farm had been established on some alluvial soil on either side of a small stream that ran into Farm Cove, planted with 'nine acres of corn'.

In 1816 Governor Macquarie completed a road, set out by his wife, that ran for three kilometres from Macquarie Street near the old Government House in Bridge Street, around Farm Cove to the point on the east side of the bay then back by a different route to Government House. The road was named by Macquarie 'Mrs Macquarie's Road', and a stone bench carved from the rock on the point where his wife used to sit to rest and admire the view he named 'Mrs Macquarie's Chair'. That same year Macquarie appointed Charles Fraser, a soldier from his 46th regiment of Highlanders to the post of 'Superintendent of the Botanic Gardens'. The gardens were renamed the Royal Botanic Gardens following the visit of Queen Elizabeth to Sydney in 1954. She was the first reigning British Monarch to visit Australia. The point where the Queen first stepped ashore in Australia in the gardens is commemorated by a sandstone wall decorated with the royal crest near the east side of the Cove.

Fort Denison

On the Harbour off Mrs Macquaries Chair is the miniature bastion of Fort Denison. Following the first court case held in Sydney on 8 February 1788, the convict Thomas Hill was found guilty of stealing biscuits from another prisoner and sentenced to a week's banishment on 'Rock Island', as it was then known, on rations of bread and water. The Island remained a convenient location for punishing recalcitrant convicts in the early days of the colony.

In November 1796 an Irish convict Francis Morgan, found guilty of a particularly brutal murder, was hanged on a gallows on Rock Island and his body left to rot in chains on a gibbet as a deterrent to others. Before he was despatched, folklore has it that upon being asked if he had anything further to say, Morgan calmly surveyed the scenery from the top of Rock Island and said, 'Well it certainly is a fine Harbour you have here.'

On the evening of 29 November 1839 two US warships led by the *Vincennes* arrived off Sydney to pay an unannounced courtesy visit. As Captain Charles Wilkes of the *Vincennes* later recalled, 'We had a fair wind for entering the Harbour and although the night was dark and we had no pilot, it was important to

Naval vessels at Garden Island during the 75th anniversary celebrations of the Royal Australian Navy in October 1986 (far right). In the background are the big guns of the American battleship U.S.S. Missouri. The Japanese surrender was signed on the deck of the Missouri in Tokyo Bay in 1945.

Garden Island naval base and Woolloomooloo Bay (right).

The American aircraft carrier U.S.S.Independence moored at Garden Island (below right).

avoid any loss of time, so I determined to run in. ...At half past ten p.m. we quietly dropped anchor off the Cove in the midst of the shipping without anyone having the least idea of our arrival. ...When the good people of Sydney looked abroad in the morning, they were much astonished to see two men o'war lying among their shipping...Had war existed, we might, after firing the shipping and reducing a great part of the town to ashes, have effected a retreat before daybreak in perfect safety.'

The surprise arrival of the warships was sufficient to prompt Governor Gipps into ordering the construction of a fort on Rock Island. The Island was quarried to the waterline but the necessary funds were not forthcoming from the British Government and it wasn't until 1855, and the onset of the Crimean War that construction to complete the Fort went ahead. The Fort was designed by Colonel George Barney of the Royal Engineers, who had been in Sydney since 1835 with

the express purpose of upgrading the defences, but had been diverted by other work such as the construction of Circular Quay and Victoria Barracks. When it was opened in 1857 the Fort was named after the Governor of New South Wales Sir William Denison.

The guns of the Fort were never fired in anger, although the fort itself accidentally once came under fire. During the Japanese midget submarine attack on Sydney in 1942, a shell fired from the American cruiser *U.S.S.Chicago* at one of the submarines, hit Fort Denison's martello tower leaving a crack that can still be seen in the top of the tower wall.

The Fort is one of the best preserved examples in the world of a martello tower. The interior of the tower, with it's three cannons that were winched in during construction because there was no way to get them in when the tower was completed, looks the same today as when the Fort was first built. Tours of Fort Denison are available by a ferry from Circular Quay.

Woolloomooloo

Woolloomooloo Bay between The Domain and Potts Point was initially known as 'Garden Cove' by the first settlers, probably because of the nearby location of Garden Island. John Palmer, accomplished dancer of the hornpipe, purser of the *Sirius* on the First Fleet and later Commissar General, was granted 40 hectares at Garden Cove in 1793 which he called 'Woolamoola Farm', no doubt the closest written description he could think of for the obscure Aboriginal name for the area. As far as the Aborigines were concerned, Woolamoola had various meanings including 'a resting place for the dead', 'where fish are caught', but most commonly 'a young male kangaroo'. Palmer later returned to England, but returned to Sydney in 1800 with his American wife and children to build a big house on his Woolamoola estate where he lived for another 20 years, becoming a wealthy ship owner, landowner and miller. In 1822 Palmer sold his estate to Edward Riley, a director of the Bank of NSW for £2,290, who shot himself dead at Woolamoola House in 1825. The main road that today carries the traffic through Woolloomooloo to Taylors Square and the airport bears Palmer's name, while Riley Street runs parallel to it two streets to the east.

Governor Macquarie called the area Henrietta Town after his wife Elizabeth Henrietta Campbell who accompanied him to Sydney, but the name never stuck, Sydneysiders apparently preferring Woolloomooloo or 'The Loo' for short.

The mudflats at the head of the bay were dredged in the 1860,s for the construction of Cowper Wharf, named after the Premier of the day Charles Cowper. The heights above Woolloomooloo were known as Eastern Hill until renamed Darlinghurst by Governor Darling. Hurst in old English meant 'a wooded hill'.

Garden Island, Australia's biggest naval base, was named within three weeks of the First Fleet landing at Sydney Cove. A note in the logbook of *HMS Sirius* on 11 February 1788 read, 'Sent an officer and party of men to the Garden Island to clear it for a garden for the ship's company.' Some of those men carved their initials on the rocks on top of the island with the date '1788'. The equivalent of the dead sea scrolls of Australia are protected under three glass pyramids.

Garden Island

In 1856 Garden Island was offered by the New South Government to the Royal Navy for use as a base in Sydney. A rigging shed, sail loft, barracks, stores and sick bay built for this purpose in the 1880's are among Sydney's best preserved colonial buildings. The figurehead of Queen Victoria in a courtyard on the base was from a wool clipper the *Windsor Castle* which plied the England - Australia trade between 1869 and 1889.

When the Royal Australian Navy was formed in July 1911, all British naval stations were handed by the Admiralty to the RAN and by extension to the Australian Commonwealth Government. In 1923, the New South Wales Government claimed the Island as it's property, a claim upheld after a seven year legal battle by the High Court. However, on the outbreak of the Second World War the Commonwealth claimed the island back under emergency wartime powers, paying £638,000 to New South Wales in 1945.

In 1938 the British Admiralty had requested that a giant dry dock be built in Sydney. By the time Garden Island was chosen as the site for the dock, it's construction had become a matter of wartime emergency. During a mammoth construction project between 1940 and 1944 employing thousands of men around the clock, Garden Island was joined to the mainland with rockfill and 330,000 cubic yards of concrete to build the Captain Cook Dry Dock. The dock, built to British plans and paid for by Australia, 1,139 feet long and 147 feet wide, was capable of dry-docking the *Queen Elizabeth* and the *Queen Mary*, at that time the largest ships in the world.

On the night of 31 May 1942 Japanese "I" Class submarines launched four two man torpedo carrying midget submarines off Sydney Heads. One was detected and attacked by a naval patrol and assumed sunk at sea, one was caught in the boom net and blown up by its crew who went down with it, but two entered the Harbour, possibly after following a vessel passing through a "gate" in the boom net. One was detected and sunk by depth charges before it could release its torpedos, the second surfaced and fired two torpedoes at the American cruiser *USS Chicago* moored to a buoy off Garden Island. One struck the shore of Garden Island without exploding, the second passed beneath a Dutch submarine lying at Garden Island, struck the Harbour bottom and exploded beneath the *S.S. Kuttabul,* a former Sydney ferry requisitioned by the Australian Navy. The Kuttabul was smashed to pieces by the force of the explosion and nineteen ratings sleeping on board were killed. They were the first and so far the last servicemen killed by enemy action in Sydney. The midget sub was immediately illuminated by searchlight and fired on by U.S. and Australian warships. Though it was never located, it is assumed to have been hit and still lying somewhere on the bottom of the Harbour, because it never returned to its mother submarine.

Two of the midget subs were recovered and their best halves welded together to make a complete submarine, which takes pride of place outside the Australian War Museum in Canberra.

One of Macquarie's place names that did endure, was Elizabeth Bay, for the bay on the east side of Potts

Point named after his wife Elizabeth Campbell.

Elizabeth Bay

The Bay is best known as the site of Elizabeth Bay House, standing in a quiet cul-de-sac on Elizabeth Bay with a view overlooking the Harbour. The unpretentious exterior gives no clue to the treasure-trove of antiques within. The domed saloon of Elizabeth Bay House and elliptical stairway are considered particularly excellent examples of colonial architecture.

In October 1826 renowned Scottish botanist Alexander Macleay arrived in Sydney to take up an appointment as Colonial Secretary accompanied by his wife and most of his seventeen children. Granted 54 acres by Governor Darling comprising all the land between present day Macleay Street Kings Cross and the shore of Rushcutters Bay, Macleay employed the architect John Verge to design a "Grecian Villa" for the site. Built between 1835 and 1838 the completed house was regarded as the finest in the colony. When the house passed out of the ownership of the Macleay Family early in the twentieth century, the rot quickly set in. A botanical garden surrounding the house was engulfed by development, the kitchen wing was demolished, and the house was successively a colony for artists, a venue for society weddings and balls, partitioned and turned into fifteen flats and finally an unused residence for the Lord Mayor of Sydney. The rot was halted in 1977, when the Historic Houses Trust of New South Wales acquired Elizabeth Bay House and painstakingly restored it to the period 1838-1845.

In 1845 when Alexander Macleay was in financial trouble, he sold the house to his son and the contents were sold to furnish the newly completed Government House. An inventory made of the contents at the time still exists, so it has been possible to faithfully reproduce the furnishings of the period.

In 1873 William John Macleay, Alexander Macleay's son's cousin, donated the family's insect, botanical, anthropological and geological collections to Sydney University where they can be viewed today in the Macleay Museum.

Other houses designed by John Verge in the area are Rockwall at the end of Rockwall Crescent, and Tusculum on the south side of Manning Street.

Around the corner at Rushcutter's Bay, hundreds of yachts are moored at the marinas of the Cruising Yacht Club of Australia.

Rushcutters Bay

In May 1788, two convicts, William Okey and Samuel Davis, sent to the swamps at the head of the Bay to cut rushes, were speared and killed by aborigines. Surgeon John White, who received the bodies when they were brought back to Sydney Cove, wrote, 'From the civility shown on all occasions to the officers by the natives, I am strongly inclined to think that

A ferry has just departed from the wharf at Darling Point in this view of the Eastern Suburbs. Pictured from left to right are Double Bay, Darling Point, Clark Island, Rushcutters Bay and Elizabeth Bay.

they must have been provoked or injured by the convicts'. Phillip travelled with an armed party by boat to the scene of the killing to examine the circumstances, concluding that 'The first injury had been offered by the unfortunate men... They had been seen with a canoe, which they had taken from one of the fishing-places.'

The creek running through the swamps at Rushcutters Bay was first crossed by a wooden trestle bridge in 1834, then by a stone arch bridge in 1839. Between 1849 and 1894 tolls were collected at a tollgate on the bay on 'New South Head Road'. The toll-keepers cottage still stands at 85 New South Head Road.

The swamp on the Bay, which originally extended over a kilometre inland, was first reclaimed for Chinese market gardens selling fruit to the city, then converted into parks and sports grounds. In Trumper Park a picturesque track beneath shady trees follows the upper course of the

original creek that ran through the swamp to the Bay. Rushcutters Bay Stadium seating 20,000 spectators, was built in 1907 for the World Heavy Weight Boxing Championship match between Tommy Burns and Jack Johnson held on Boxing Day 1908. The stadium was still used for holding boxing tournaments until

1970, when it was pulled down during construction of the Eastern Suburbs Railway.

Darling Point

Naval buildings on the east side of Rushcutters Bay, were once the site of the headquarters of the New South Wales Volunteer Naval Brigade,

formed in 1863. Their moment of glory came in June 1900, when 260 men from the brigade were sent to China to assist in putting down the Boxer uprising. By the time they arrived the trouble was over and after some token policing duties the brigade returned to Sydney with no casualties in April 1901. During their absence Australia had become a federation, so they departed as volunteers of the New South Wales Naval Brigade and returned as volunteers of the Australian Navy. Some intricately carved woodwork they souvenired while in China is now in the Powerhouse Museum at Darling Harbour.

Yarranabe Park on the shore of the east side of Rushcutters Bay, and Yarranabe Road, winding above the west and north shore of the headland, are named after the local aboriginal tribe that inhabited the area. Their last camp site was on the high ground near the junction of New South Head Road and Ocean Avenue

Previous pages: Double Bay and Darling Point with Sydney City in the background.

Redleaf Pool and Seven Shillings Beach at Double Bay with Rose Bay in the background (far right).

Clarke Island and Point Piper (right).

Double Bay. Here, old Wingle, his wife Kitty, and Bondi Charley demonstrated boomerang throwing to a crowd of onlookers for copper coin or the occasional crown.

Major General Ralph Darling, Governor of New South Wales from 1825 to 1831 named the headland 'Mrs Darlings Point' after his wife, a name which soon became abbreviated to simply Darling Point. The point remained virtually uninhabited until the first bridging of the creek through the swamps of Rushcutters Bay in 1834. Two enormous nineteenth century houses built on the point are of particular interest. On Darling Point Road a battlemented mansion called

the Swifts, built originally for the owner of the Castlemaine Brewery, was until recently the official residence of the Catholic Archbishop of Sydney. Nearby Bishopscourt on Greenoaks Avenue was built in 1847 as the home of Thomas Sutcliffe Mort and was renamed 'Bishopscourt' when it became the residence of the Anglican Archbishop of Sydney. Michael Guilfoyle, a gardener employed on Mort's property, bought three and a half acres of land in the centre of Double Bay and established an 'Exotic Nursery' which he lovingly maintained for twenty three years from 1851 to 1874. He introduced many plants to Australia, including

the South American jacaranda, camellias and azaleas. Guilfoyle Avenue in Double Bay marks the boundary of his garden.

Clarke Island

A pre-arranged water-taxi from the wharf at Mckell Park at the end of Darling Point Road is a good point of embarkation for nearby Clarke Island. The pickup must be phoned through in advance to one of the Sydney water taxi companies. No permission is needed to visit the Island, which has a fresh water supply, toilets, picnic areas, and a path around the perimeter and through the copse of woods at the top. Lieutenant Ralph

Clarke of the First Fleet had a vegetable patch on 'Clarke Island'. According to his diary, on 18 February 1790, 'After I was relieved from guard, I went down to my island to look at my garden and found that some boat had landed since I had been there last and taken away the greatest part of a fine bed of onions. I thought that, having a garden on an island, it would be more secure, but I find that they even get at it there.' On 21 March Clarke's diary continued, 'Soon after breakfast, I went out in my boat, down to my island, and found that some person had been there again and had taken away all my potatoes. Whoever they are, I wish

they were in hell for their kindness.' Today the island is part of Sydney Harbour National Park administered by the New South Wales Parks and Wildlife Service.

Double Bay

Frantic shoppers at the ritzy shopping centre of Double Bay - or 'Double Pay' as it is frequently called - seem more interested in emptying the contents of their wallets, than in the twin beaches of Double Bay and Seven Shillings Beach between Darling Point and Point Piper. However the mood changes on sunny weekends when picnickers and sunbakers frequent Double Bay Park and

Redleaf Pool on Seven Shillings Beach. Redleaf, one of Sydney's most picturesque harbourside pools, is accessible by a path and some steps through Redleaf Gardens at 536 New South Head Road. The gardens have won several awards for their well maintained presentation. Woollahra Council Chambers at Redleaf House next door maintain a library book exchange program with it's 'sister' suburb of St Cloud in Paris.

Harbourside parks and sheltered beaches

See the Harbour's longest beach and visit beautiful Nielsen Park and Sydney's best known historic home, Vaucluse House. Dine at famous Doyle's Restaurant and stroll the cliff-top path at The Gap. Swim at the beaches of Watsons Bay or walk to Hornby Lighthouse on South Head at the south entrance to the Harbour.

Point Piper

John Piper from Ayrshire Scotland arrived in Sydney in February 1792 with the New South Wales Corps, then spent a considerable portion of his early career in the antipodes at Norfolk Island penal settlement, where he was for a time acting commandant. On Norfolk Island he met and married Mary Ann Shears, the daughter of a convict, who travelled with him when he returned to Sydney. In 1814 Macquarie made Piper 'Naval Officer of Port Jackson' with the responsibility of collecting customs dues and levies on shipping for a salary of £400 a year plus a commission of 5% on all funds collected. Due to an extraordinary unexpected rise in the volume of shipping coming into Sydney, Piper's income rose to over £4,000 a year, a fortune when one considers that Harbour Master Robert Watson at nearby Watsons Bay was receiving a quite reasonable annual salary of £50 a year.

Piper received extensive land grants in the vicinity of Woollahra, where he owned a vast estate covering much of Sydney's eastern suburbs including Vaucluse. In 1816 he embarked on the construction of a mansion on Point Piper costing £10,000 which took four years to complete. There 'the Prince of Australia' as he became known, spared no expense entertaining his friends, who were brought from Sydney Cove in his own longboat, accompanied by an immaculately dressed band of pipers, playing highland airs to soothe them on the journey. To get to work at his office in the Argyle Centre in The Rocks, Piper had a hand-built carriage pulled by four Arab thoroughbreds from his stables where he also lavished funds on establishing breeding stock and racing horses.

When Governor Darling arrived in Sydney in 1825 he examined Piper's affairs, found he had been 'neglectful' in collecting customs dues and dismissed him from his post. Piper's world came crashing down around him. Forced to sell his Point Piper mansion and other properties including Vaucluse House, Piper decided to put an end to his troubles and was rowed out by his boatmen into the Harbour off Point Piper, and while one of his pipers played a final lament he jumped overboard. Hauled from the water unconscious by his boatmen and revived, his friends managed to scratch together enough from his ruined estate to buy a property near Bathurst. Soon in financial trouble again, Piper died near Bathurst at another property aged 78 in 1851.

Point Piper is in the Municipality of Woollahra, aboriginal for 'camp' or 'meeting place'. Woollahra House, built in 1871 on Point Piper, was pulled down by developers in the

Previous pages: The magnificent vista of Sydney Harbour from Watsons Bay.

Point Piper (left) with the broad crescent of Rose Bay on the right and Shark Island on the left.

1930's, but it's gatehouse, close to Rose Bay Park on the corner of Wanulla Road and New South Head Road is occupied by a minuscule Police Station. Nearby, opposite Wolseley Road on the other side of New South Head Road is Cranbrook, a mansion originally built by the merchant and shipowner Robert Towns, then used as a temporary residence of the Governor of New South Wales from 1902 to 1917 while Government House on Farm Cove was 'lent' to the Australian Governor General. Since 1918 Cranbrook has been one of Sydney's best boys schools.

Shark Island

Shark Island, 250 metres long by about 100 metres wide, 500 metres off Woollahra Point, was used in the late nineteenth century as an animal quarantine station. Now a public reserve as part of Sydney Harbour National Park, permission to visit the Island should be sought from the National Parks and Wildlife Service. The pavilion on top of the Island dates to 1911. A schooner called the Newcastle ran aground on Shark Island in 1826. It was repaired at Darling Harbour but sank a month later on the central New South Wales coast near the city which now carries its name.

Rose Bay

The two kilometre crescent of Rose Bay on the east side of Point Piper is the longest beach on the Harbour. The Bay was named by Governor Phillip after George Rose (Lord Sydney), Secretary of the Home Department, who chose Phillip to lead the First Fleet expedition to Botany Bay.

Ever since the pioneering days of manned flight, Rose Bay has been associated with flying contraptions. Lawrence Hargrave, whose head appeared on the first 20 dollar notes, lived at 58 Wunulla Road Point Piper. He built many models of aeroplanes

Lady Martins Beach, Point Piper (above).

Point Piper and the Harbour looking west (right).

and aeroplane engines and used to test his designs over Rose Bay. He contributed papers on aerodynamics to journals all around the world and among his many achievements is credited with inventing the box-kite. Four kites built by Hargrave lifted a man 16ft from the ground at Stanwell Park south of Sydney on 12 November 1894.

Lyne Park on the shore in the middle of Rose Bay, was Sydney's main international airport from 1938 to the 1950's. From the 'Sydney Water Airport' as it was called, 'Empire' and 'Sunderland' flying boats operated by Qantas and Imperial Airways offered services to Singapore and the U.K., and across the Tasman Sea to New Zealand. After the fall of Singapore in 1942, the flying boats were pressed into wartime service, including the transport of over 24,000 troops from Australia to New Guinea. The flying boat base is thought to have been the target of a Japanese submarine, which surfaced off Bondi on the night of June 7 1942 and shelled Rose Bay before being driven off by coastal guns. Of the 7 shells fired, 5 failed to explode, and the only casualty was a civilian with a broken leg. A light flying boat still operates from the wharf at Lyne Park offering joy flights over the Harbour and flights to Palm Beach and Gosford. The grand old flying boats of the old days are remembered by Sunderland Avenue in Lyne Park.

Nielsen Park

Bayview Hill Road in Vaucluse near the east end of Rose Bay is the starting point for a foreshore walk that leads to Nielsen Park and Vaucluse House and returns via New South Head Road to Bayview Hill Road. The walk could be done in two hours, or occupy the best part of a day, with a stop for a swim and lunch in Nielsen Park and a tour of Vaucluse House. Park on Tivoli

Shark Beach (top) at Nielsen Park. There hasn't been a fatal shark attack in the harbour since 1963, but just in case Shark Beach has a netted swimming enclosure in the Summer. On Steel Point in the foreground are the remains of an 1870's gun emplacement.

The Sacred Heart Convent (above left) overlooks Rose Bay from Bayview Hill on the east side of the Bay.

Milk Beach and the grounds of Strickland House (above) are accessible from the Hermitage Walking Track which follows the east shore of Rose Bay.

Shark Island (above right), completely deserted on a weekday, is crowded with picnickers at weekends.

Avenue off Bayview Hill Road. Towering above like a medieval castle is the Sacred Heart Convent, originally a mansion built by a Sydney merchant George Thorne in 1851. Bought by the Catholic Church in 1882, the convent stands in 8 hectares of grounds including tennis courts a swimming pool and a chapel built in 1900.

The track, known as the Hermitage Foreshore Track after a large Victorian gothic style house built in 1837 called the Hermitage standing above the track near Hermit Point, starts at the bottom of Bayview Hill Road. The trail winds up and down past three small beaches, Queens Beach, Tingara Beach and

Milk Beach, with brilliant views across to Shark Island and the city, to reach after about a kilometre Strickland House. The grounds of the house, which are open to the public, are accessible from the track or via Vaucluse Road. Strickland House was originally built in 1854 by John Hosking the first Mayor of Sydney, who named the house 'Carrera' after the marble fireplaces imported from Carrera in Italy, then it was renamed after Lord Strickland, Governor of New South Wales during the First World War when the house was used as a military hospital. Hosking's call to riches was through his marriage to the daughter of ex-convict Samuel Terry, a publican and

moneylender who became a large landowner by foreclosing on mortgages.

Not far beyond Milk Beach a branch track leads to 40 metre high 'Mt Trefle' in Nielsen Park, a pocket of the original Sydney Harbour bushland and the only known location of a recently discovered species of casuarina tree. Continuing on the foreshore track as it enters Nielsen Park, on a low headland at Steel Point are the remains of some gun emplacements carved out of the solid rock in 1871.

Nielsen Park is named after Neil Nielsen, a strong supporter of the so-called Foreshore Vigilance Committee, formed at the beginning of the twentieth century to urge the government to make available for public use private land around the harbour foreshores. Neilsen, Minister for lands in the State Government of 1910-13 authorised the purchase of 30 acres of harbourside land for a park from the former Vaucluse estate in 1912. Neck to knee swim-suits were all the rage when the kiosk, bathing sheds, toilets and showers at the park were built in 1914. The grassy slope above the east side of the beach with a beautiful view down the harbour to the city and Opera House must rate as one of the best places on the Harbour for a picnic. The gothic style Greycliffe House in the park was completed in 1852 for John Reeve, the husband of William Wentworth's daughter Fanny. During recent restoration of the house a secret passage built of hand-cut sandstone blocks was discovered leading from the cellar to a deep well, then by a side passage to an exit on the eastern side of the garden.

Vaucluse House

From Nielsen Park walk along Coolong Road and across Wentworth Road to Vaucluse House.

Vaucluse House was given it's name by an Irish Baronet, Sir Henry Brown Hayes, Sheriff of Cork and

Between the arms of Vaucluse Point on the left and Laings Point on the right (below) are from left to right, Vaucluse Bay, Parsley Bay and Watsons Bay. Manly and North Head are in the background.

Vaucluse House (right).

Vaucluse Bay and Vaucluse Park (below right). Vaucluse House and stables are in the park at the lower right of the picture.

Captain of the local militia. 'The Gentleman Convict' as Hayes was known, transported for abducting a Quaker heiress and forcing her to marry him, was despatched to Sydney on board the convict transport *Atlas*, arriving in July 1802. With money brought out from Ireland Hayes was permitted by Governor King to buy 200 acres of land near South Head for £100 from Thomas Laycock, Quartermaster of the New South Wales Corps, to establish a farm. Employing fellow convicts to cut down trees and clear the ground, Hayes called his property 'Vaucluse' after Fontaine de Vaucluse in France, located in a similar setting in a steep sided valley and itself named from the Latin vallis clausa for 'enclosed valley'.

Hayes built a stone cottage on the site surrounded by a trench which his convicts filled with earth imported in barrels from Ireland to keep out the snakes. Pardoned in 1812, Hayes returned to Ireland and the house and land became for a time the property of John Piper before being bought by William Wentworth. (See also the Wentworths at Homebush Chapter 5). In 1803 when he was thirteen William had been sent by his father D'Arcy to England, where he received a thorough classical education at a school in Bexhill, Sussex, returning to Sydney in 1810 aged nineteen.

When he bought the Vaucluse estate, William kept Hayes' original stone cottage, as the living room of a new much larger home, completed with fittings, decorations and furnishings that were the best money could provide. The house has now been restored to the condition it was in when occupied by the Wentworths in about 1840. A visit today is as much a celebration of the life of William Wentworth, as a visit to a historic house. William Charles was one of the greats of Sydney's early colonial days, as an explorer, author, barrister and statesman, who's achievements epitomise the Australian ideal that it doesn't matter where you come from (he was a bastard conceived on the transport *Neptune* to a convict mother transported for stealing clothes), but what you do that counts. In his role as a barrister and statesman he was instrumental in drawing up the terms of the first constitution of New South Wales, which was drafted at Vaucluse House.

William lived at Vaucluse from 1827 with his wife Sarah and children until departing for England in 1853. When he died in England in 1872 aged 82 his body was brought back to Australia, he was given a state funeral and his remains were interred in a vault on the Vaucluse estate (the Wentworth Chapel, in nearby Fitzwilliam Road).

Continue south behind Vaucluse House through the grounds to a flight of steps climbing out of the head of the valley next to a stream. Cross Olola Avenue and continue up some more steps to Hopetoun

Avenue, named after Lord Hopetoun, the first Governor General of Australia from 1901-03. Turn right on Hopetoun Avenue from where it is about a ten minute walk along New South Head Road to return to the car on Tivoli Avenue.

Watsons Bay

A four kilometre drive back along Hopetoun Avenue past another very pleasant harbourside park at Parsley Bay takes you to Watsons Bay. The bay is named after Robert Watson Quartermaster of the *Sirius* of the First Fleet. After being posted to the Signal Station on the nearby cliffs in 1791, then working as Harbourmaster controlling the pilot boats at Watsons Bay until sacked for 'stealing a quantity of canvas', Watson was made the first Lighthouse Keeper when the Macquarie Lighthouse started operations in 1816 and maintained the light until he died in 1819.

Watsons Bay is still the base for pilot boats in Sydney. In the early

Gibsons Beach at centre left and Kutti Beach on the right at Watsons Bay (left).

Parsley Bay (below left) has a netted swimming area, a pedestrian suspension bridge over the water and a shady park on the flat ground at the head of the Bay.

Doyle's seafood restaurant on the water at Watsons Bay (right) has been owned and operated by the same family for over 100 years.

A view of Watsons Bay from the Harbour (below).

days pilots living in huts at Camp Cove would frantically row out to ships entering the port in the hope of being first to a vessel to bargain with the captain to navigate their ship up the harbour. The captain had the option of carrying on without a pilot if he didn't want to pay, until 1833 when it became compulsory for ships unfamiliar with the Harbour to take on a pilot before entering the port. For many years the pilots risked life and limb rowing out to ships outside the port in open whaling boats in all weathers. On 20 July 1867 pilot Robinson was attempting to board the full-rigged sailing ship the *Strathdon* in a southerly gale when his boat capsized. Robinson drowned with four men of his crew and four men from other boats, two of which capsized attempting a rescue. These days the modern day motorised orange and blue pilot boats moor at the pilot station next to the harbourside baths at Gibsons Beach Watsons Bay.

Watsons Bay used to be the first port of call in Sydney for sailing ships entering the Harbour. Merchants and officials would travel out to the Bay on Old South Head Road to pick up the mail, conduct customs procedures and collect the cargo manifest.

From the harbour beach at Watsons Bay it's a 250 metre walk to the 'Dunbar Memorial Lookout' above the cliffs at The Gap. The worst ever single tragedy to take place in Sydney occurred at the Gap on the night of 20 August 1857 when the migrant ship the *Dunbar* was blown onto the rocks below in a gale. No one saw the ship strike the rocks and it wasn't until the following morning with spray from the surf blowing over the top of the cliffs that the wreckage was sighted. Out of the 122 on board only one man, Able Seaman James Johnson, survived by clinging to a rock ledge where he was spotted 36 hours after the ship went down and rescued by rope. Johnson was later appointed lighthouse keeper at Nobbys Head at the entrance to Newcastle harbour. The ship's anchor recovered in 1907, is set in concrete at the edge of the cliff.

When the tram line from the city opened at Watsons Bay the terminus was at Gap Road, literally within spitting distance of the cliffs of The Gap. Possibly due to the morbid attraction of the location following the tragedy of the Dunbar, the Gap became a favourite spot for suicides. So much so that tram (and later bus) conductors, noticing any melancholy passengers travelling on their own to Watson's Bay, would remonstrate with them to try to divert them from a drastic course of action, many of whom were quite satisfied with their earthly lot.

Nearby St Peters Church of England designed by Edmund Blacket and completed in 1864 was built on the hill with the hope it would be the first building to greet the eyes of passengers arriving in Sydney by ship. According to a brass plaque at the back of the church, the organ, built by Robert and William Grey of London in 1796 was used by Napoleon when he was exiled on St Helena. The Greycliffe Memorial Gates at the church were erected in memory of those who lost their lives in the Greycliffe ferry disaster.

Camp Cove

Back on the Harbour side of Watsons Bay, 400 metres from The Gap along Military Road and Cliff Street is Camp Cove. In January 1788 when Phillip landed at Botany Bay he found the area swampy and unsuitable for settlement with no deep water anchorages for ships. On leaving Botany Bay in 1770 Captain Cook had sailed north two miles off the coast, and had mentioned in his journal 'a Bay or Harbour where there appeared to be safe anchorage which I called Port Jackson (lying) 3 leagues to the northward of Botany Bay'. On the afternoon of January 21 1788 Phillip set out with three long-boats to explore Port Jackson. His expedition arrived off the harbour in the evening, rounded South Head, and set up camp for the night at 'Camp Cove' watched by a party of 'natives' on the nearby high ground who set up a chant and waved their spears. In Green Park on Laings Point at the west end of the beach a plaque on a memorial commemorates the fact that Camp Cove was the first place where white people stepped ashore in Sydney.

Hidden away among the grass and shrubs of the park on Laings Point are an old gun emplacement, command post and storehouse. A tunnel entrance, now concreted up, not far from an old stone navigation marker on the shore, was the entrance to some passageways beneath the point. The boom net to prevent enemy shipping entering the harbour during the Second World War had it's southern end anchored at the point.

South Head

From Camp Cove a forty minute return walk leads to South Head. At the north end of the cove, walk up some wooden steps to an old road paved with sandstone slabs next to a 'firing wall' with rifle slots and follow it to a gun emplacement containing a cannon on an iron carriage manufactured by W.G. Armstrong & Co

Camp Cove was the first place where white men stepped ashore on Sydney Harbour.

Bathing costumes are voluntary at Lady Bay Beach (below).

The old lighthouse keepers cottages and Hornby Lighthouse on South Head (right) have commanding views of Sydney Harbour.

Another view of Lady Bay (opposite page bottom left) with the buildings of HMAS Watson training base in the background.

Hornby Lighthouse (opposite page below right). Next to the lighthouse a World War Two concrete lookout post gazes across to the cliffs of North Head.

Newcastle on Tyne in 1872. Keep to the path on top of the rocks to Lady Bay Beach.

For years Lady Bay had been an unofficial nudist beach when in 1975 it was suddenly raided by the police who arrested 35 men and woman out of a total of about 200 nudists on the beach and charged them with indecent exposure. An appeal by a man against his conviction was upheld by a Criminal Appeals Court Judge and a cabinet subcommittee was set up to look into the matter. After careful deliberation the government made Lady Bay an 'official' nude bathing beach the following year.

Continue on the track to reach South Head after a further ten minutes walk. Scattered about the head are old fortifications dating from the nineteenth century to the Second World War. South Head was originally fortified in 1859 amidst concerns the Americans may raid the town to steal the fortune in gold accumulating in Sydney banks during the goldrush. The work was speeded up on the outbreak of the American Civil War when there were fears the North may declare war on England for aiding the Southern States. At the tip of the head stands the red and white striped Hornby Lighthouse, completed in 1858 after the tragedy of the Dunbar. The lighthouse was named after Sir Phipps Hornby, Commander In Chief of the British Pacific Fleet. A ship which has the lighthouse on its port beam is considered to have entered the harbour.

Manly Jetcat has just departed it's berth at Circular Quay in this view of the City and Opera House.

Map Section

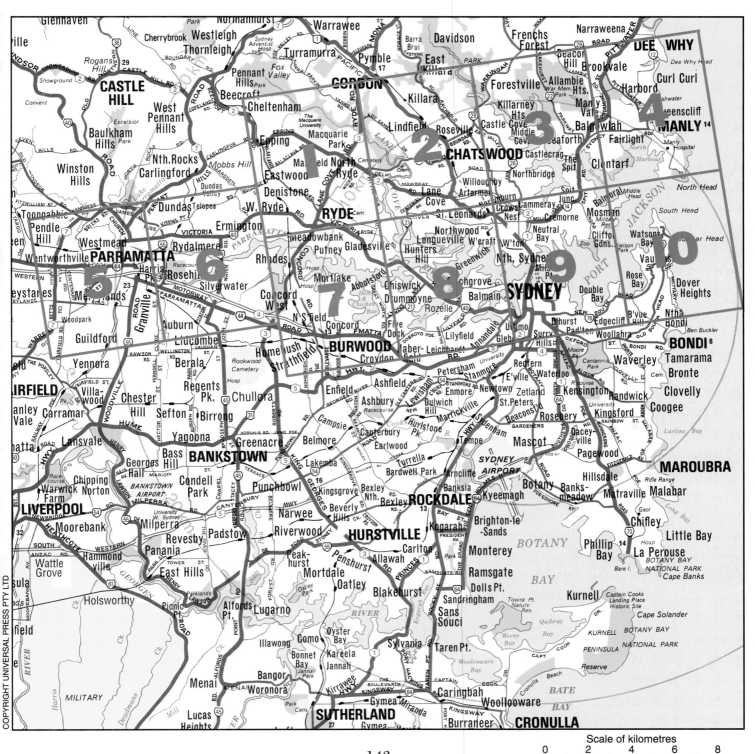

Scale of kilometres
0 2 4 6 8

MAP 1

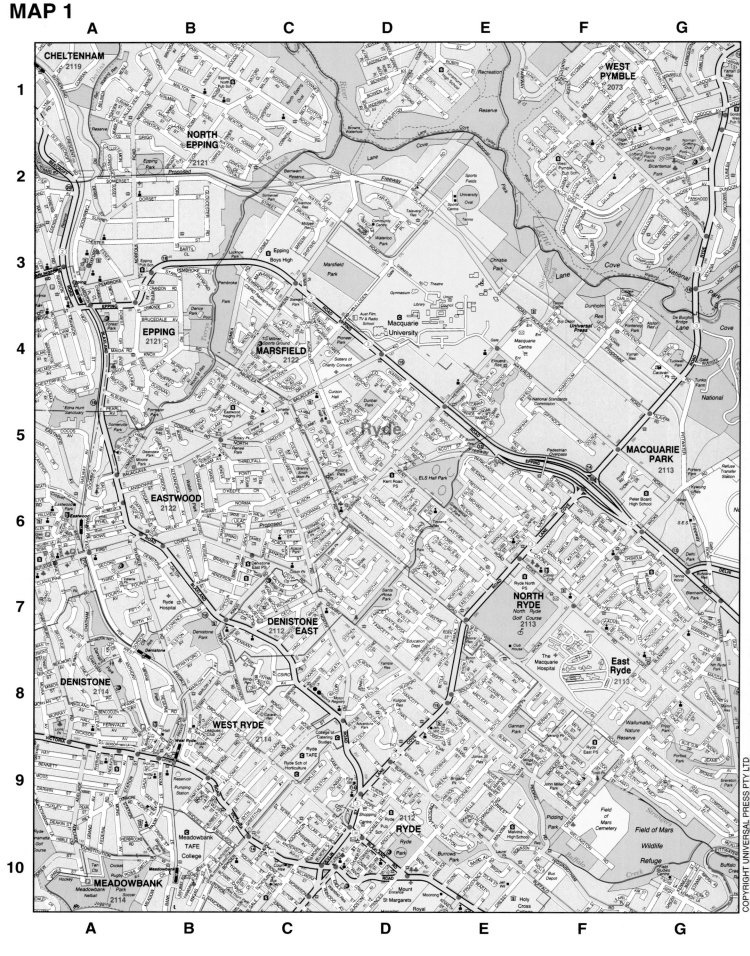

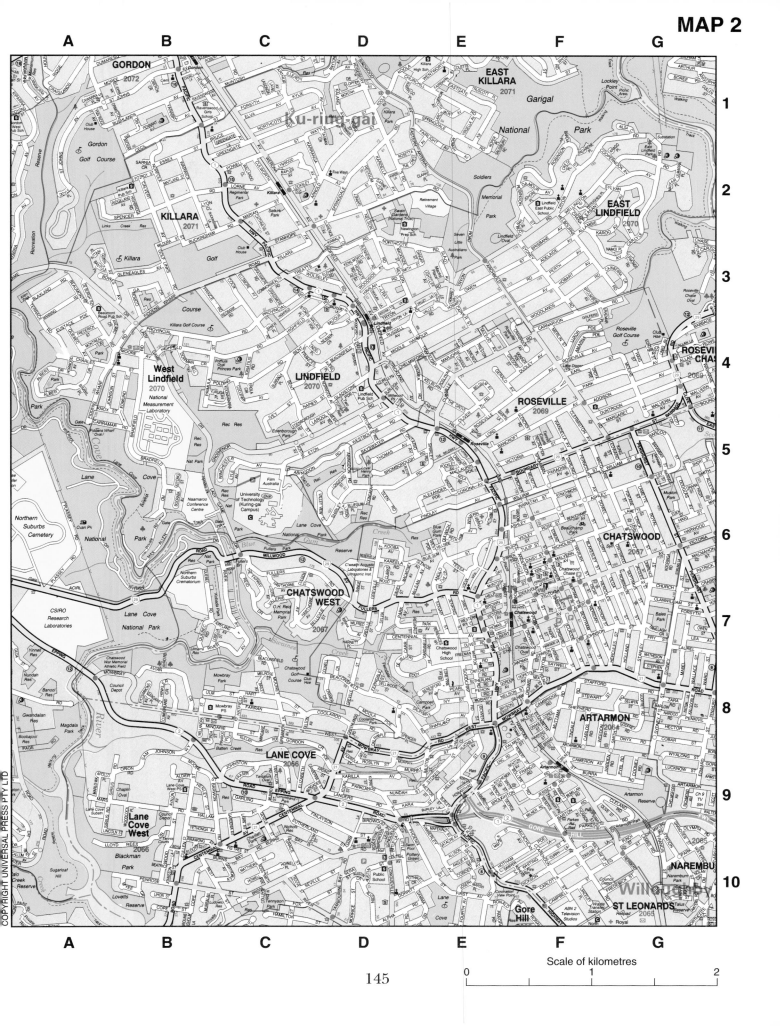

MAP 2

Scale of kilometres

MAP 3

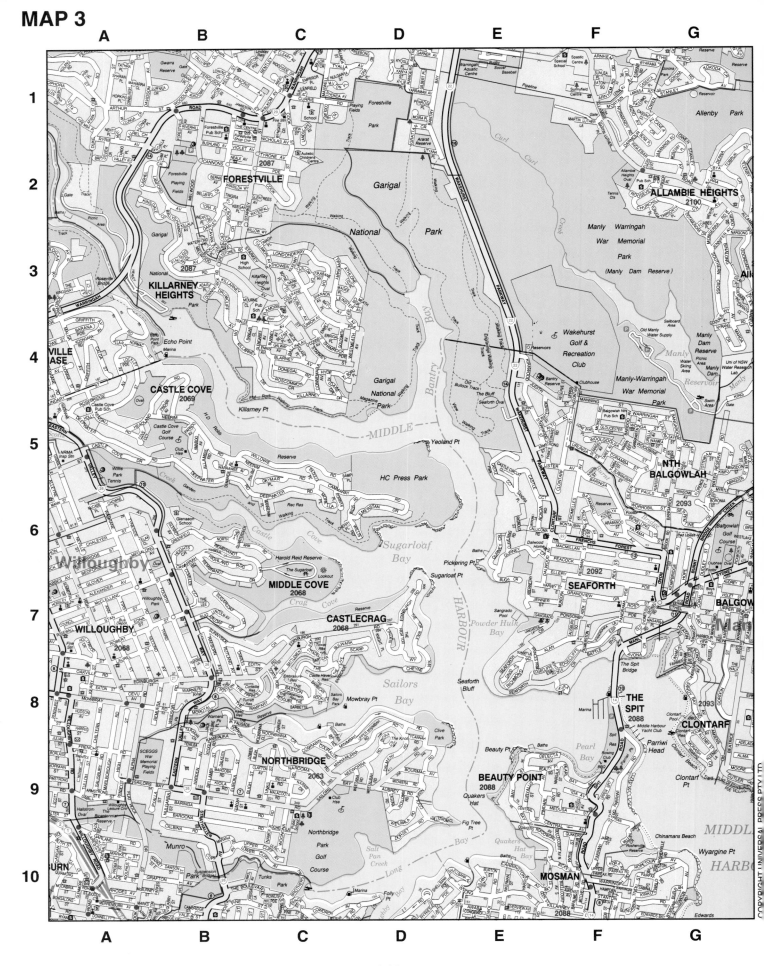

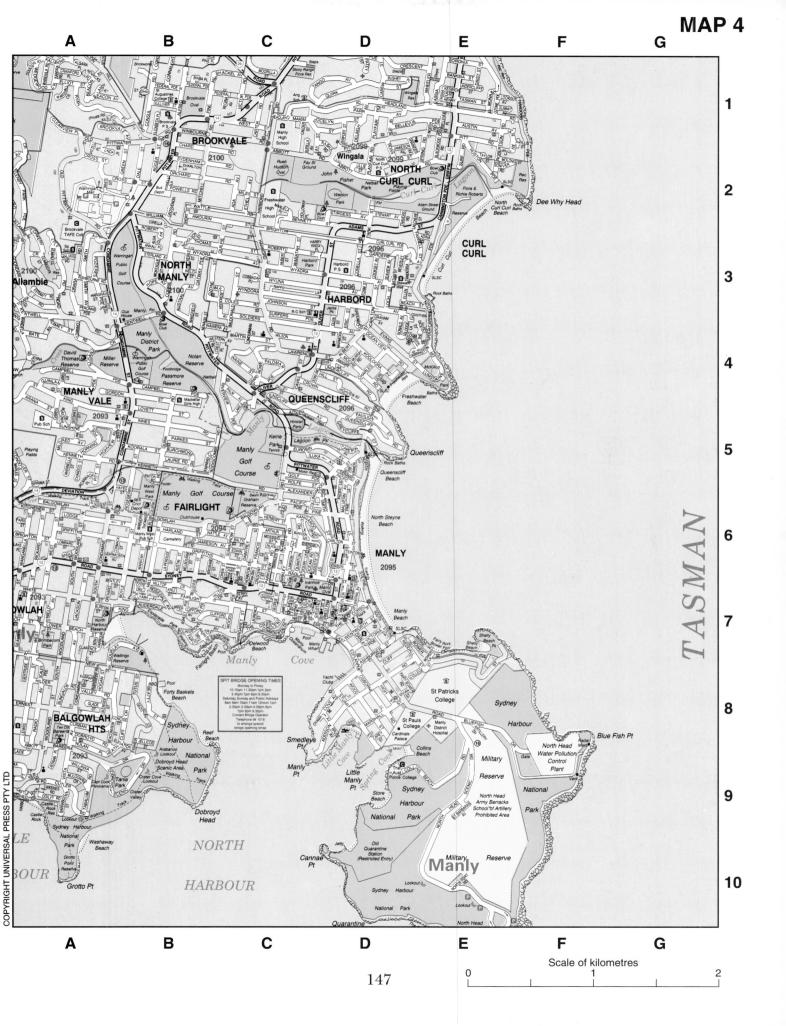

MAP 4

SPIT BRIDGE OPENING TIMES
Monday to Friday
10.15am 11.30am 1pm 2pm
2.45pm 7pm 8pm 9.30pm
Saturday, Sunday and Public Holidays
8am 9am 10am 11am 12noon 1pm
2.30pm 3.30pm 4.30pm 6pm
7pm 8pm 9.30pm
Contact Bridge Operator
Telephone 94 1018
to arrange special
bridge opening times

TASMAN

NORTH HARBOUR

Scale of kilometres
0   1   2

MAP 5

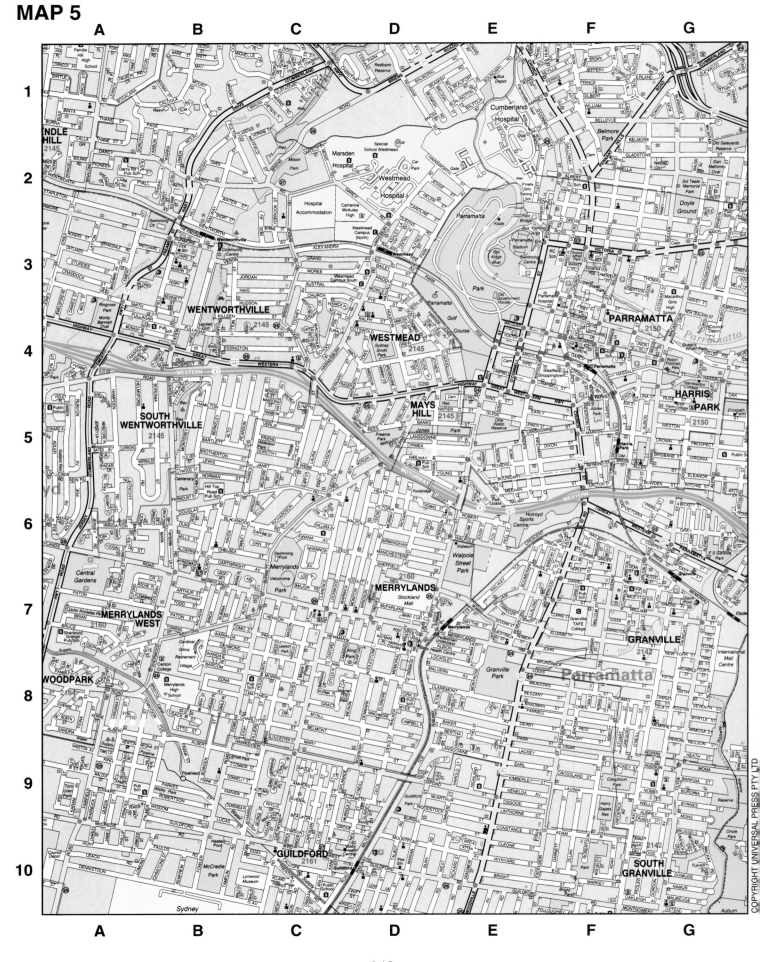

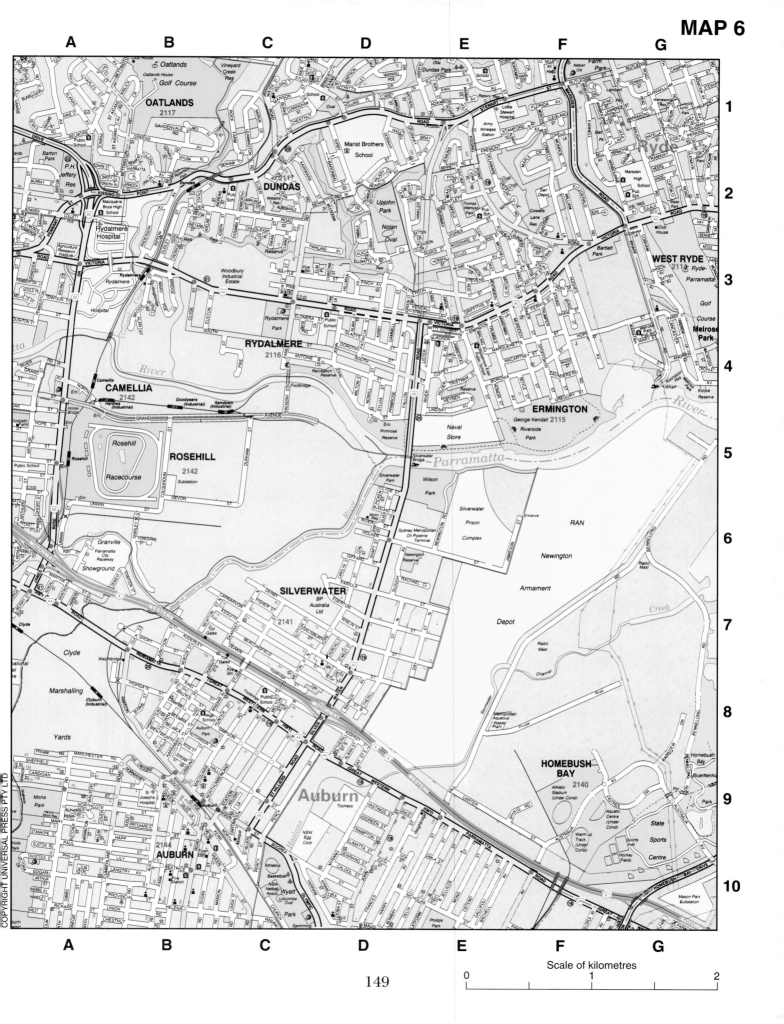

MAP 6

Scale of kilometres

0   1   2

MAP 7

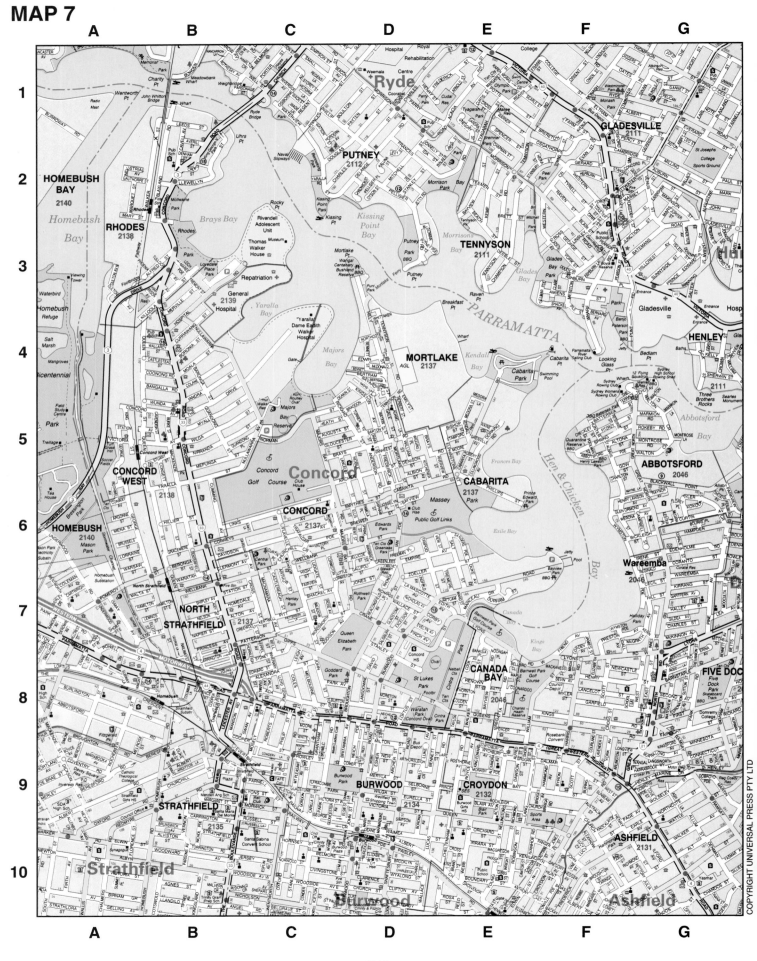

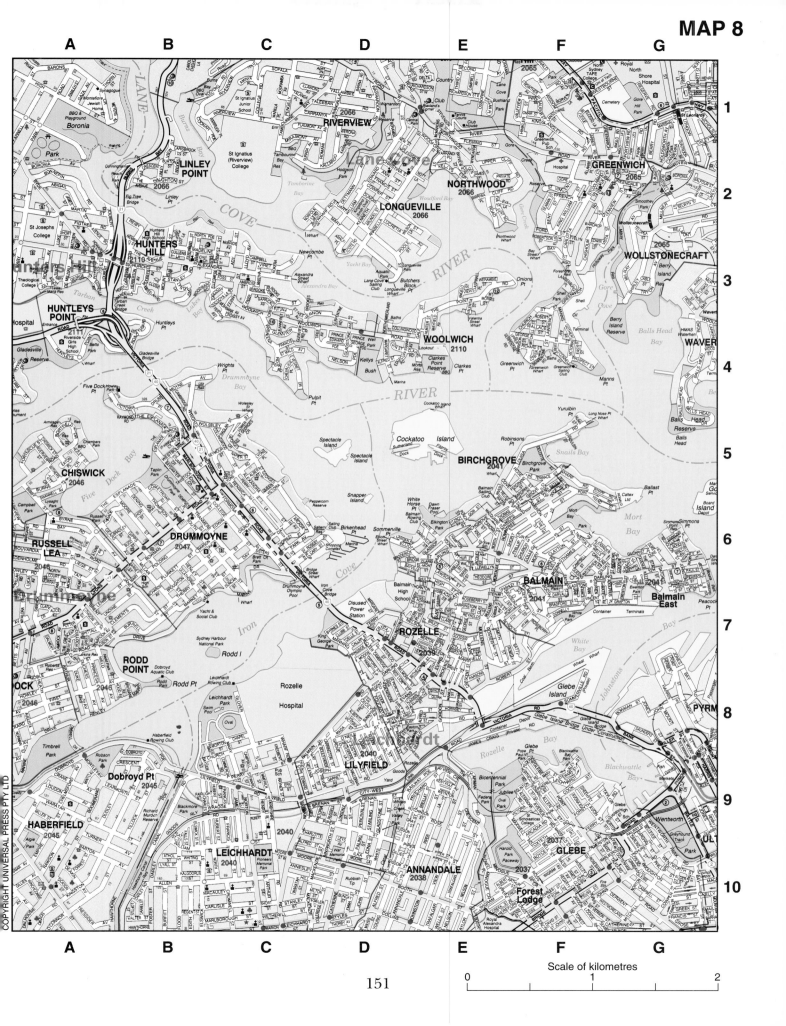

MAP 8

MAP 9

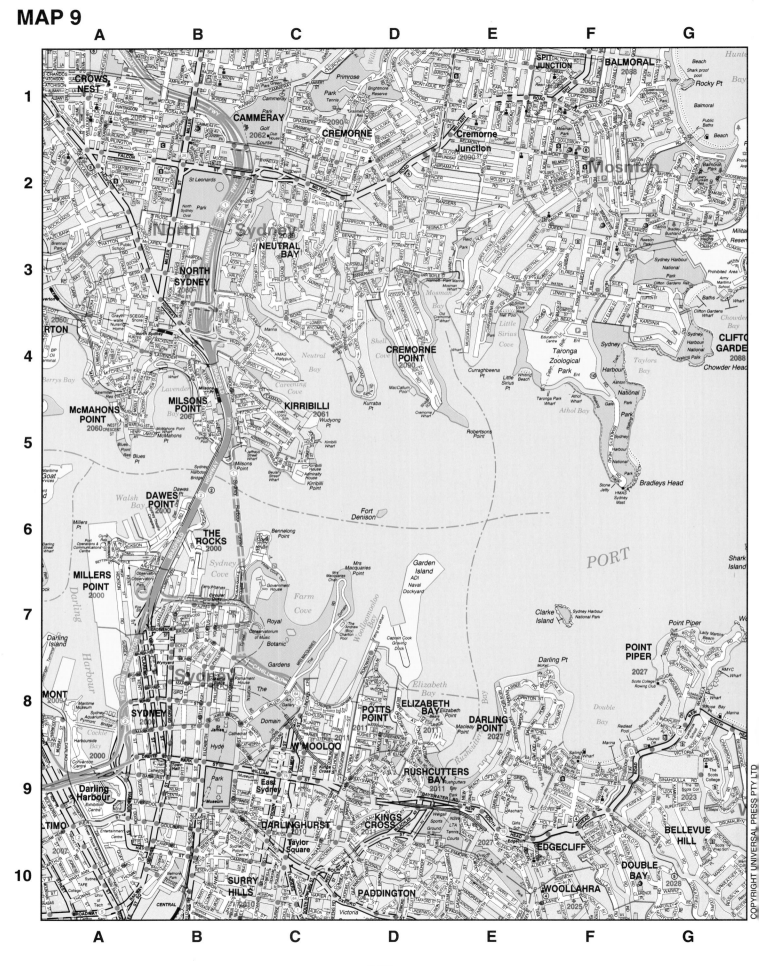

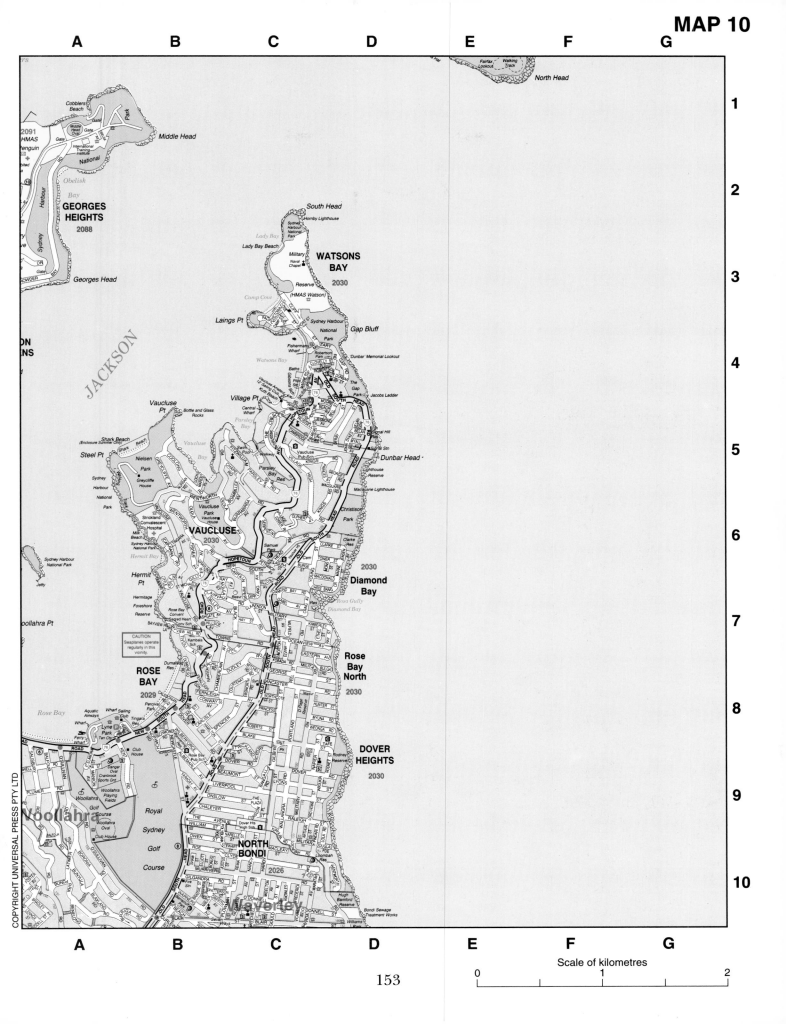

MAP 10

North Head

South Head

GEORGES HEIGHTS
2088

WATSONS BAY
2030

JACKSON

VAUCLUSE
2030

Diamond Bay
2030

Rose Bay North
2030

ROSE BAY
2029

DOVER HEIGHTS
2030

Woollahra

Royal Sydney Golf Course

NORTH BONDI
2026

Waverley

Scale of kilometres

0   1   2

Index

Acknowledgements

Pat Wright, Wayne Vardanega, Rob Haylock and David Gemmell of Sydney Helicopter Service, and John Barnao of Helicopter Charter, who always put the helicopter in the right position to get the picture that was required. Almost all the pictures were taken from a Robinson R22 helicopter and the few exceptions from a Bell Jetranger.

Pentax 6 x 7 cameras using 90mm and 45mm lenses were used to photograph all the pictures in the book. Fuji 50 ASA Velvia slide film was used for nearly all the photos, with the remainder shot on Kodak Ektachrome EPR 64 slide film.